Machine Learning

The ultimate beginners guide to learn Machine Learning, artificial intelligence & neural networks step-by-step

Mark Reed

Table of Contents

Introduction

Over the years, machine learning has become one of the pillars of information technology and a large part of our lives. With the ever-increasing amounts of data becoming available, there is more reason to believe that smart data analysis will be more prevalent as an integral part of technological progress. Machine learning has come a long way due to the incredible amount of new computing technologies developed every day. While the science behind machine learning has been around for a long time, it has gained fresh momentum in recent years with the development of better computers and more efficient systems. This has led to an increase of people who want to know what machine learning is. Of course, that is why you picked up this book.

Have you ever wondered how your computer is able to filter out spam in your emails, how Amazon makes recommendations on what products to buy, or how Netflix tells you what shows you should watch next? All of this is achieved through machine learning. When you look for something through a search engine, machine learning is what brings you the relevant results. One of the more important applications of this technology is fraud detection. By learning your patterns, fraud detection can determine if any given activity is suspicious or not. Truly, machine learning is in every part of our lives.

You may be thinking, "I'm interested in machine learning but I don't have a background in computer science or mathematics. Therefore, I might not be able to understand and work any of the techniques used in machine learning". This is a fairly common sentiment among beginners and it has put a lot of people off from pursuing machine learning. However, there is no need to fear. Anyone can grasp machine learning, as well as the involved the tools and techniques. While a background in fields such as computer science, programming, statistics, calculus, and other forms of higher-level math may be beneficial, it is not always required. Or if it is, it is typically at a more superficial level than people think.

The purpose of this book is to provide you, the reader, with an overview of what machine learning is and the vast range of applications that utilize various machine learning problems, and thus provide you with a better understanding of it all. As a beginner, you need a good foundation in machine learning in order to know what's vital as you advance your knowledge. This book provides a simplified approach to machine learning by breaking it down into simple, easy-to-understand bits. This will make it easier to retain what you learn for longer. And, going forward, you will always have this book to use as a reference.

In chapter one, we will refresh our knowledge on some machine learning fundamentals such as what machine learning is, why it is important, and its uses. We will also take a look at the main classes and base concepts of ML (machine learning) systems.

In chapter two, we will take a look at how to deal with data in ML systems. We will discuss how data is processed, from loading it to wrangling it. We will also examine how different types of data (such as text, images, numerical data, etc.) are handled.

Chapter three will explore the classification of data in machine learning—how to train a classifier, different classification algorithms, and error analysis.

Chapter four will teach you how to train models using various algorithms. We will also take a look at support vector machines.

In chapter five, you will learn how to evaluate different ML models and how to pick the most appropriate one for your needs.

Chapter six will deal with dimensionality reduction and its importance.

In chapter seven, we will take a look at neural networks and deep learning, and how they apply to machine learning. This chapter will also cover neural nets and their uses, important neural net architectures, deep neural net training techniques and more.

At the end of each chapter, there will be a summary of everything we discussed as well as a handful of exercises to help you internalize these concepts.

After reading this book, you should have a basic understanding of what machine learning is. An important lesson you will learn while studying ML and other forms of programming is that it pays to have patience. Some of the concepts can take time to get the hang of, and you can very easily lose your enthusiasm. However, just as it takes time for a computer to process and understand data, it will take time for you to fully understand these concepts. Creating computer models and algorithms that analyze and learn from data, in conjunction with studying and learning from human interaction, is no easy task. Thus, you need to be patient as you learn and build your knowledge in this field. In the end, your patience will pay off.

Chapter One:
Machine Learning Fundamentals

Many people associate machine learning with robotics (robotic butlers or helpers, toys, etc.). However, machine learning is no longer a futuristic concept. From the early applications of the OSR (optical character recognition) to its more known application, the spam filter, machine learning has come a long way. Now, this technology powers hundreds of applications that we use every day.

You may be wondering where machine learning actually starts, or even where it ends. What does it mean for a machine to learn? How does it learn? If I searched for something on Google, has my computer learned something from the search results? Did it become smarter? In this chapter, we will tackle what machine learning is, its importance, and the basics of how it works.

What is Machine Learning?

Machine learning is the art of programming computers so they can learn from data. Arthur Samuel, the American technology pioneer who popularized the term, defines machine learning as: "the field of study that gives computers the ability to learn without being explicitly programmed."

11

Tom Mitchell, a professor at Carnegie Mellon University and author of *Machine Learning* (1997), offers a more recent explanation of this technology. "A computer program is said to learn from experience E with respect to some class of tasks T and performance measure P, if its performance at tasks in T, as measured by P, improves with experience E."

Let us take your spam filter, for instance. It is a machine learning program that learns to flag spam emails from given examples, such as emails flagged as spam by other users and by examining the format of non-spam emails. This system that uses examples to learn is referred to as The Training Set. Every example is referred to as a Training Instance. In this case, the task labeled T is used to filter new emails, and the experience E makes up the training data that the performance measure P requires to be defined— using the ratio of correctly classified emails, for instance. This specific performance measure is referred to as Accuracy and its applied in classification tasks.

Why Use Machine Learning?

Machine learning has come a long way because of new computing technologies. Researchers interested in AI (artificial intelligence) wanted to know if computers could learn from data. As a result, the technology evolved from pattern recognition and the postulation that machines can learn without being programmed to carry out certain tasks. The repetition aspect of ML is crucial because, as models are subjected to new data, they can adapt independently. They learn from preceding computations to produce reliable, replicable decisions and results. This means that ML has a wide variety of applications.

Let's come back to spam filtering. If you had to write a program that filters spam emails using conventional programming techniques, it would be very tedious. You would have to write an algorithm to detect patterns in emails commonly flagged as spam, such as identifying certain key words like "Amazing", "Just for you", and so on. You would then have to repeat this process, adding rules to the algorithm to help it detect spam as it evolves to get around detection software. Maintaining this algorithm will become taxing over time.

On the other hand, a spam filter based on ML techniques automatically learns what phrases or words are indicators of spam and detects patterns in flagged emails compared to non-spam emails. This ML program is shorter to write, easier to maintain, and much more accurate. It is able to detect changes to common words and phrases, thus flagging spam emails without your intervention.

This is one of the many practical applications of machine learning. You can use ML techniques to tackle problems that are too difficult for conventional approaches or that lack a known algorithm, such as speech and pattern recognition. With the growing amount and variety of data, we need computational processing that's cheaper, more powerful, and that allows for affordable data storage. This means that we can create models that analyze larger and more complex datasets to provide accurate results faster and more efficiently. To create a good machine learning system, your data has to be well-prepared. You will need algorithms that are both simple and advanced enough to process the data. You have to be able to automate and repeat processes to improve the accuracy of the program, ensemble models, and ensure that your system is accessible.

Types of ML Systems

There are various kinds of machine learning, but most can be grouped together based on one of two things:

- If they need to be trained with human supervision or not. These include supervised, unsupervised, semi-supervised, and reinforcement learning. If the system can learn incrementally or on the fly—through online or batch learning, respectively.

- If they work by comparing new data to old data, or if they find patterns in training datasets and create a predictive model—whether it is instance-based or model-based learning.

These criteria aren't mutually exclusive and you can combine them in any way you want. For example, a modern spam filter can learn as it goes using deep neural network models trained using examples of non-spam and spam emails. This is an example of an online, model-based supervised learning ML system.

1. Supervised Learning

As stated before, ML learning systems can be grouped as per the amount of data they process and the kind of supervision they need during training. In supervised learning, the training datasets that you feed the algorithm include the desired solutions, referred to as labels. Normal supervised learning tasks are called classifications. Using the earlier example of a spam filter program, it is trained using a variety of emails and their classes (i.e. spam vs. non-spam), and it must learn how to group incoming emails. Another simple task is predicting a target numerical value, like the price of a house is given a set of features (location, size, current market value, etc.) referred to as predictors. This kind of task is known as regression. In order to train this system, you would need to input a lot of examples of houses on the market, their predictors, and their labels.

IMPORTANT TIP: in ML, an attribute is a concrete type of data (such as house size), while a feature can have a variety of meanings as per the context. Generally, an attribute refers to the data's value (e.g. house size = three bedrooms). However, these terms are often used interchangeably. In ML, a target is called a label while in statistics, a target is called a dependent variable. A variable in statistics is referred to as feature in ML, and a transformation in statistics is called feature creation in ML.

Please note that there are regression algorithms that can also be utilized for classification and vice versa. Take logistic regression, for instance. It is commonly utilized for classification because it can provide a value that matches the probability of a particular class (e.g. an email having a 30 percent chance of being spam).

Through methods like classification, regression, prediction, and gradient boosting, supervised learning utilizes patterns to foretell the values of the label on unlabeled data. Supervised learning is often used in applications that use historical data to predict future events. For example, it can anticipate fraudulent credit card transactions or predict which customer is likely to buy a certain product. Examples of supervised learning algorithms include k-Nearest Neighbors, linear regression, logistic regression, support vector machines, decision trees, random forests, and neural networks. You should note that there are some neural network architectures that are unsupervised, like autoencoders and restricted Boltzmann machines. They could also be semi-supervised, such as those used in deep belief networks and unsupervised pretraining.

2. Unsupervised Learning

This is used for data that has no historical labels (i.e. the system is not told the desired outcome). The system has to figure out the desired outcome on its own. The goal of this learning method is to explore data and find patterns or some structure within. It works especially well with transactional data. For instance, the algorithm can identify customers with similar attributes who can be treated the same in marketing campaigns or find attributes that distinguish customers from each other. Popular techniques include k-Means, hierarchical cluster analysis (HCA), and expectation maximization for clustering. Principal component analysis (PCA), kernel PCA, locally-linear embedding (LLE), t-distributed stochastic neighbor embedding (t-SNE) for visualization and dimensionality reduction and for association rule learning, Apriori, and Eclat. These algorithms are also utilized in dividing text topics, recommend items, and identifying data outliers.

Let's say that you have a lot of data from the user base of customers on your website. You could run a clustering algorithm to help group your client base into separate categories. At no point are you telling the algorithm which customer belongs in which group. The system does this on its own. If you have a blog and you notice that about 35 percent of your readers are women who love cooking while 20 percent are young food enthusiasts, you could use a hierarchical clustering algorithm that would divide each group into smaller ones. This would aid you in creating posts that target each group specifically.

Visualization algorithms are fed complex unlabeled data and present a 2D or 3D representation of data that can be easily plotted. They try to maintain as much structure as they can by keeping the inputted data clusters from overlapping in the visualization. This helps you understand how the algorithm organized the data and, possibly, how to detect unsuspected patterns.

Dimensionality reduction is a related task that tries to simplify data without causing too much data loss. You can do this is by merging correlated features. For instance, an automobile's mileage can be related to its age, so a dimension reduction algorithm can help merge these datasets into a feature that represents the vehicle's wear and tear. This is referred to as feature extraction.

IMPORTANT TIP: it is highly recommended to run your data through a dimension reduction algorithm before feeding it into another algorithm. Not only will this help the second algorithm run faster, but the data will occupy less hard drive and memory space. This process will also help the system perform better.

Anomaly detection is another crucial unsupervised task that can be used to identify instances of credit card fraud, manufacturing anomalies, or to automatically remove outliers from a dataset before using this data in another algorithm. Since the anomaly detection algorithm is trained using normal instances, it can easily tell whether a new instance is normal or not.

The goal of associate rule learning, another common unsupervised task, is to dig into large datasets and pinpoint intriguing relations between the attributes. As an example, let's say you own a mini mart. Running an association rule algorithm on your sales logs can show you, for instance, customers that purchase barbecue sauce also tend to purchase steaks. Therefore, you could generate more sales for both items by placing them close to each other.

3. Semi-supervised Learning

In semi-supervised learning, algorithms handle labeled data, partially labeled data, and a large percentage of unlabeled data. A good example of this kind of learning is photo hosting services such as Google photos. After uploading your photos, it can detect that a particular person (Person A) is in four of the uploaded pictures and that someone else (Person B) is in three. The unsupervised section of the algorithm is what clusters similar data together. The next step is for you to tell the system who Persons A and B are.

These labels are quite useful when it comes to searching for photos. Many semi-supervised algorithms are comprised of both unsupervised and supervised algorithms. Unsupervised restricted Boltzmann machines (RBMs) make up deep belief networks (DBNs). The RBMs are trained sequentially in an unsupervised manner and the whole system is fine-tuned using supervised learning methods.

4. Reinforcement Learning

This type of learning system is very different from the others. The learning system referred to as an Agent can observe, select, carry out actions, and get rewarded or penalized. The system has to learn by itself what the best strategy, called a policy, is to get rewarded. The policy determines the action the agent should take in a given situation. One example of reinforcement learning is DeepMind's AlphaGo program that became world champion in Go after beating Lee Sedol. It developed its winning strategy after analyzing many games and playing itself. The learning algorithm was turned off during the match so the machine only applied the winning strategy it learned.

5. Batch Learning

Another criterion used to classify ML systems is whether or not they can learn on the fly or sequentially. In batch learning, the system cannot learn incrementally. It has to be trained using all the available data. This process can use up a lot of computing resources and can be time consuming, so it is often done offline. The system is trained, then runs without learning anything new. It simply applies what it has learned in a process called offline learning. If you want a batch system to learn new data, you have to train a new system with both the new and old data. Then, once it is ready, replace the old system with the new one. Luckily, this whole, training, evaluating, launching, and ML system process can be automated quite easily. This way, even batch learning systems can adapt to changes.

Batch learning is a simple solution that works most of the time, but you would have to train a new system daily or weekly by using this process. If you need a system that adapts to data changes quickly, such as predicting stock prices, you need a more reactive solution. If you have a system that learns autonomously but has limited resources, such as a smartphone app storing huge amounts of data and using up most of the computing resources, this process may not be right for you.

6. Online Learning

Online learning is an easy solution to the issues attached with batch learning. With online learning, you can train your system gradually by inputting data instances sequentially one-by-one or in small groups called mini-batches. Each step in the learning process is fast and cheap so the system can learn new data as it comes in. This type of learning is great for systems that receive data continuously (e.g. stock prices) and needs to adapt fast or autonomously. It's a great option if your resources are limited because it doesn't need to store the new data once it has learned about new data instances, unless you choose to store it. This saves a lot of disk spaces. Online learning is used to train systems that require huge datasets that cannot fit into the machine's memory. This is referred to as out-of-core learning. The algorithm loads some of the data, runs a training step on it, and repeats the process until all the data is done.

A vital parameter of these systems is how rapidly they should adapt to data changes. This is called learning rate. The higher the learning rate, the faster the system will adapt to new data. An unfortunate side-effect is that it forgets old data just as fast. You don't want a spam filter to only flag the latest kinds of spam and forget the older forms. However, if you set a low learning rate, your system will learn slowly and be less attuned to noise in the new data and sequences of data points.

A big downside to online learning is that if the system is fed bad data, its performance will decrease gradually. In the case of a live system, your clients or users will notice. An example of bad data could be a malfunctioning sensor on a robot. To limit the risk, you need to watch your system closely and quickly turn off the learning or revert to a previous working point if a performance drop is detected. Also, keep an eye on the input data to detect any abnormalities. One way to do this is by using an anomaly detection algorithm.

7. Instance-based Learning

ML systems can also be categorized by how they generalize data. A lot of these systems are used to make predictions. This means that when the system is given a couple of training examples, it should be able to generalize similar examples it has never seen before. Even having a good performance measure on training datasets is insufficient because the true purpose of the system is to perform well with new instances. In instance-based learning, the system learns by heart, then generalizes new cases using the same measure. If you built a spam filter this way, it would flag emails that are similar to those previously flagged as spam. While this is not the worst solution, it is definitely not the best.

Not only should spam filter should flag similar emails, but it should also be programmed to recognize emails similar to known spam. A measure of similarity is required between the two emails—by counting the number of similar words they have in common, for instance. The system should flag this email as spam if it has too many words in common with a spam email.

8. Model-based Learning

Another way to generalize examples is by building a model from these examples and using it to make predictions. Within the last few decades, researchers have built thousands of ML algorithms. An engineer who wanted to conventionally solve a problem using ML had to choose one or more of the various algorithms at their disposal, or they had to try to invent a new one. In essence, their selection of algorithm was restricted to those algorithms they knew or were familiar with. The availability of particular software also affected their algorithm choices, and they would not have been the best choice for their specific problem.

The model-based approach, however, seeks to produce a bespoke solution tailored to every new use. Instead of transforming your problem to fit a standard algorithm, model-based machine learning allows you to create the algorithm precisely to fit your problem. This framework was created using three key ideas: the adoption of a Bayesian viewpoint, use of factor graphs (which are probabilistic graph models), and the application of quick, defined, efficient, and estimated inference algorithms.

The core idea of model-based machine learning is that assumptions about the problem domain are made explicit in model form. A model is comprised of this set of assumptions expressed in mathematical form. These assumptions can include both the number and kind of variables in the problem domain, which variables influence each other, and what effect changing one variable has on another.

Model-based Machine Learning (MBML) Key Ideas

- Bayesian Inference

In MBML, hidden parameters are represented as random variables with probability distributions. This provides a more understandable and principled style of quantifying the changes in the model parameters. Once the examined variables in the model are set to their observed values, originally assumed probability distributions are updated using Bayes' theorem.

This is in contradiction to the conventional ML framework, where parameters for models are designated average values defined by optimizing an objective function. Bayesian inference on large ML models with millions of variables is likewise implemented using Bayes' hypothesis in a more complicated manner. This is because this theorem is an exact inference technique that is intractable over large sets of data. In recent years, the improvement of computer processing power has enabled the research and development of quicker and more efficient inference algorithms that are scalable to extensive data such as Belief Propagation (BP), and Variational Bayes (VB).

- Factor Graphs

Probabilistic Graphical Models (PGM),

particularly factor graphs, are the next component of MBML systems. A PGM is a diagrammatic depiction of the cumulative probability distribution over randomized variables in a model displayed as a graph. Factor graphs are a kind of PGM that comprise of circular nodes showing random variables, vertices for conditional dependencies between nodes, and square nodes for the conditional probability distributions (factors). They present a general framework for illustrating the joint distribution of a set of randomized variables.

In factor graphs, latent parameters are treated as random variables, and they learn their probability distributions by utilizing Bayesian inference algorithms along the graph. Learning is solely the product of factors over a subset of variables in the graph. This allows for the effortless implementation of local message-passing algorithms.

- Probabilistic Programming (PP)

Probabilistic programming (PP), is a new revolution in computer science where programming languages are created to compute with uncertainty in addition to logic computing. This means that current programming languages can now support random variables, constraints on variables, and inference packages. Using a PP language, you can define a model of your problem in a compressed form with some lines of code. Then an inference engine automatically generates inference routines (and even source code) to work out that problem. Some notable examples of PP languages include Infer.Net, Stan, BUGS, church, and PyMC.

There are three steps to model-based machine learning, namely model description. Model description is where you define the process that produces the data using factor graphs, the condition of the observed variables to their known quantities, and performance inference. This performs backward reasoning to update previous distributions over latent parameters.

Model assumptions play an important role since computer learning cannot produce solutions wholly from data alone. There are always assumptions constituted into any algorithm, although they are far from exact. Different algorithms communicate with varying sets of assumptions and, when they are implicit, the only way to ascertain which algorithm provides the best results is to analyze them empirically. This is time-consuming and ineffective, and it needs software implementations of every algorithm compared against each other. And if none of the algorithms you've analyzed offer the desired results, it becomes even harder to figure out how to formulate a better algorithm.

Challenges Faced When Using Machine Learning

Since the main objective is selecting a learning algorithm and training it with data, you will encounter two main problems: bad data and bad algorithms. Let's start by taking a look at challenges that arise from using bad data.

1. Insufficient Training Data

When you teach a child what an orange is, you have to show them what it is and tell them that what they're looking at is an orange. Eventually, the child will be able to tell what an orange is. Unfortunately, machine learning has not evolved to such stages yet. It requires a ton of data for most algorithms to work properly. Even for simple tasks, you will require tons of data. And with complex problems such as facial recognition, you will require millions of examples.

2. Non-representative Training Data

In order for a system to generalize data well, it's essential that your training data represents the new cases you want to generalize, too. Using training sets that are representative of the cases you want to generalize is harder than it sounds. If your sample set is too small, you will end up with sampling noise, which is a non-representative dataset as a result of chance. However, even large dataset samples can result in noise if the sampling method is flawed. This is referred to as sampling bias.

3. Poor Data Quality

If your training data is loaded with errors, noise, and outliers due to something like poor measurement quality, it becomes harder for such a system to detect hidden patterns and thus less likely to perform well. Therefore, it is very important to take the time to clean up your training data. For example, discarding or fixing instances that are very clearly outliers can help the system function better. If you are missing some features, you must decide whether you want to ignore this attribute altogether, or if you want to ignore the instances instead and fill in the missing values with median values. Or, alternatively, train one model with the feature and another without.

4. Irrelevant Features

Your ML system will learn only if the training data contains enough relevant features and fewer irrelevant ones. Coming up with a reliable set of features to train your system is an integral part of creating any successful ML project. This process is called feature engineering and it involves selecting, extracting, and creating new features. You have to pick the most useful features to train your system from the existing ones. Then, you have to combine them to create a more useful system—dimension reduction algorithms can help here. Finally, create new features by gathering fresh data. The following issues arise from the use of bad or flawed algorithms.

5. Overfitting training data

Let's say you visit a foreign city and you get conned by a taxi driver. You could be tempted to say that all taxi drivers in that city are con artists. Overgeneralizing is something human beings have a tendency to do, and this can translate to machines if you are not careful. In ML this is referred to as overfitting, and it means that the model performs well in training but doesn't generalize well. Overfitting occurs when the ML model is too complex compared to the noise and amount of training data used.

To rectify this, you can simplify the model using fewer parameters—using a linear model instead of a polynomial model, or decreasing the number of attributes in the training datasets and constraining the model. You can also gather more training data to improve accuracy and reduce the noise in the data by fixing errors and eliminating outliers.

Regularization is the act of constraining a model to simplify it and lessen the chance of overfitting. For example, a linear model has two variables, $\theta 0$ and $\theta 1$. This provides the algorithm with two degrees of freedom to adjust the model to the training data by tweaking either the height ($\theta 0$) or slope ($\theta 1$) of the line. If θ1 = 0, the algorithm would have a singular degree of freedom, making fitting the data much harder. This is because the algorithm can only slide up and down the line when trying to get as close to the data instances, meaning it would settle at the mean of the instances.

If we modified θ1 to a value but kept it small, the algorithm would have somewhere between one and two degrees of freedom to work. This model would still be a simple model, just more complex than the previous one. You want the right balance between keeping the model simple and fitting the data perfectly to ensure it generalizes well.

The amount of regularization you should apply can be managed by a hyperparameter. This is a parameter of a learning algorithm, not the model, and therefore must be set before training starts. It should remain constant throughout, even though it is unaffected by the algorithm itself. If you set the hyperparameter to a high value, the slope of the graph will be almost flat or closer to zero. Even though the algorithm is less likely to over fit the data, it will also not offer a good solution. The tuning of these hyperparameters is an essential part of creating an ML system.

6. Underfitting the training data

This is the exact opposite of overfitting and it

takes place when your models are too simplistic to learn the underlying data structure. For instance, if you use a linear model to showcase life satisfaction, it is prone to underfit because reality is more complex than the model shows. Thus, its predictions will be inaccurate, even with the training data. To fix this issue you can, pick a stronger model with more parameters, input better variables to the algorithm, and reduce model constraints by decreasing the regularization hyperparameter.

Chapter Summary

- We defined Machine Learning as a branch of artificial intelligence focused on making machines better at specified tasks by learning from data instead of explicit code rules.
- There are various types of machine learning systems such as supervised, unsupervised, batch, online, reinforcement learning, and more.
- In an ML project, you collect data in a training set and input this training set into a learning algorithm. If the algorithm is model-based, it adjusts parameters to fit the model to the training set (such as making accurate predictions on the training dataset itself). Hopefully, it can then make predictions on new instances as well. If the algorithm is instance-based, it learns the examples by heart

and applies a similarity measure to generalize fresh instances.

- The ML system will not perform well if either your training dataset is too small or if it's not representative, noisy, or flawed with irrelevant features (garbage in, garbage out).

- Your model should strike a balance between being too simplistic, thus underfitting the data and too complex which can result in overfitting.

Exercises

This chapter was a refresher course on machine learning fundamentals and other important concepts. Here are some exercises to help you internalize what you learned.

A. How would you define Machine Learning?
B. Can you name an area where machine learning is applied?
C. What is a labeled training dataset?
D. Name two (2) common supervised tasks.
E. Name four (4) common unsupervised tasks.
F. What kind of ML algorithm would you utilize to enable a robot to walk in different, unfamiliar terrains?
G. Would you classify spam detection as a supervised or unsupervised learning problem?
H. Define out-of-core learning.

I. Differentiate between a model parameter and a learning algorithm's hyperparameter.

J. What do model-based learning algorithms look for? Name common strategies they use to succeed. How do these algorithms make predictions?

K. Name some of the main challenges in Machine Learning.

L. If your model performs well while using training data but generalizes poorly to new instances, what is happening? Name three possible solutions for this.

Chapter Two:
Dealing with Data in Machine Learning

The very first step in any ML project is getting raw data into our systems. This data can be from a log file, dataset file, or a database, among other sources. The quality of an ML model heavily depends on the data it is fed. The data collected from mining can sometimes have missing values and is susceptible to containing noise. This results in poor data quality, which in turn produces a bad model. In this chapter, we will take an in-depth look at how to handle data in ML systems, from loading data to wrangling it, and how to handle different types of data. First, we will take a look at loading data from various sources such as CSV files and SQL databases, and cover ways of generating simulated data with the desired properties required for experimentation. Since python is the most popular programming language choice for ML frameworks and libraries, we will use it going forward. There are many types of loading data in the Python ecosystem. We will focus on using the Pandas Library's large set of techniques for loading external data. We will also use Scikit-learn, an open-source machine learning library in Python, for creating simulated data.

Loading a Sample Dataset

This is how you load a preexisting sample dataset using Scikit-learn. Scikit-learn has several popular datasets you can use:

```python
# Load scikit-learn's datasets
from sklearn import datasets

# Load digits dataset
digits = datasets.load_digits()

# Create features matrix
features = digits.data

# Create target vector
target = digits.target

# View first observation
features [0]

array([   0., 0., 5., 13., 9., 1.,
0., 0., 0., 0., 13.,
         15., 10., 15., 5., 0., 0.,
     3., 15., 2., 0., 11.,
          8., 0., 0., 4., 12., 0.,
     0., 8., 8., 0., 0.,
          5., 8., 0., 0., 9., 8.,
     0., 0., 4., 11., 0.,
```

```
       1., 12., 7., 0., 0., 2.,
    14., 5., 10., 12., 0.,
        0., 0., 0., 6., 13., 10.,
    0., 0., 0.])
```

You don't want to have to load, transform, and clean real-world data before you can utilize it in a learning algorithm or method. Fortunately, Scikit-learn comes with preloaded datasets referred to as toy datasets, that you can easily load. This is because they are smaller and cleaner than real-world datasets. Some other popular datasets include load_boston, which contains 503 observations on Boston housing prices and it makes a great dataset to test out regression algorithms. The load_iris dataset contains 150 observations on the measurements of Iris flowers. This dataset is great for investigating classification algorithms. The load_digits dataset has 1,797 observations from images of handwritten digits. It is great for teaching image classification.

Creating Simulated Datasets

Scikit-learn provides several ways for creating simulated data, and these three methods are particularly useful. If you want to use the dataset with a loner regression algorithm, then make_regression is a great choice.

Load library

```
from sklearn.datasets import
make_regression

# Generate features matrix, target
vector, and the true coefficients
features, target, coefficients =
make_regression(n_samples = 100,
      n_features = 3,
      n_informative = 3,

      noise = 0.0,

      random_state = 1)

# View feature matrix and target vector
print('Feature Matrix\n', features[:3])
print('Target Vector\n', target[:3])

Feature Matrix
[[ 1.29322588 -0.61736206 -0.11044703]
[-2.793085 0.36633201 1.93752881]
[ 0.80186103 -0.18656977 0.0465673 ]]
Target Vector
[-10.37865986 25.5124503 19.67705609]
```

If you are interested in building a simulated dataset for classification, you can use make_classification:

```
# Load library
from sklearn.datasets import
make_classification
```

```
# Generate features matrix and target
vector
features, target =
make_classification(n_samples = 100,

        n_informative = 3,

        n_classes = 2,
        weights = [.25, .75],


# View feature matrix and target vector
print('Feature Matrix\n', features[:3])
print('Target Vector\n', target[:3])

Feature Matrix
[[ 1.06354768 -1.42632219 1.02163151]
 [ 0.23156977 1.49535261 0.33251578]
 [ 0.15972951 0.83533515 -0.40869554]]
Target Vector
[1 0 0]
```

Finally, if you want a dataset created to work properly with clustering techniques, you can use make_blobs:

```
# Load library
from sklearn.datasets import make_blobs

# Generate feature matrix and target
vector
```

```
features, target = make_blobs(n_samples
= 100,
    n_features = 2,
    centers = 3,
    cluster_std = 0.5,
    shuffle = True,
    random_state = 1)

# View feature matrix and target vector
print('Feature Matrix\n', features[:3])
print('Target Vector\n', target[:3])

Feature Matrix
[[ -1.22685609 3.25572052]
 [ -9.57463218 -4.38310652]
 [-10.71976941 -4.20558148]]
Target Vector
[0 1 1]
```

From the solution, it is clear that make_regression returns a feature matrix of float values and a target vector of float values too, while make_classification and make_blobs return a feature matrix of float values and a target vector of integers showing membership in a particular class. Scikit-learn datasets provide broad options for managing the type of data that is generated. Its documentation has a full description of all parameters. Here are some that are worth noting:

- In the make_regression and make_classification tools, n_informative defines the number of features that are utilized to produce the target vector. If it is less than the total amount of features (n_features), the resulting dataset will have redundant features identifiable through feature selection techniques.

- Make_classification has a weight parameter that enables us to simulate datasets with imbalanced classes. For instance, weights = [.25, .75] would produce a dataset with 25% of observations pertaining to one class and 75% of observations pertaining to a second class. For make_blobs, the centers parameter defines the number of generated clusters.

Using the matplotlib visualization library, you can envision the clusters generated by make_blobs:

```
# Load library
import matplotlib.pyplot as plt

# View scatterplot
plt.scatter(features[:,0],
features[:,1], c=target)
plt.show()
```

Loading CSV Files

If you want to import a comma-separated-values file, you can use the Pandas library read_csv to load a local or hosted CSV file:

```
# Load library
import pandas as pd

# Create URL
url                                     =
'https://tinyurl.com/simulated_data'

# Load dataset
dataframe = pd.read_csv(url)

# View first two rows
dataframe.head(2)
integer    datetime          category
0 5         2015-01-01        00:00:00 0
1 5         2015-01-01        00:00:01 0
```

When loading CSV files, there are two things to note: First, it is useful to examine the contents of a file quickly before loading. It can be beneficial to see how the dataset is structured beforehand and what variables you are required to load in the CSV file. Secondly, read_csv has over 30 parameters, so its documentation can be daunting. Luckily, these parameters are there to allow the algorithm to handle a wide assortment of CSV formats. For instance, CSV files are so named because commas separate the values (e.g., one row might be 2, "2015-01-01 00:00:00",0). However, it is fairly common for "CSV" files to employ other characters as separators, such as tabs.

Pandas' sep parameter permits you to define the delimiter used in the file. Sometimes, a common formatting issue with CSV files is that the first line of the file represents column headers (such as the integer, datetime, or category in the above example). The header parameter enables us to clarify if and where a header row exists. If one doesn't exist, set header=None.

Loading Excel Files

This is done using pandas library's read_excel:

```
# Load library
import pandas as pd

# Create URL
url =
'https://tinyurl.com/simulated_excel
'

# Load data
dataframe = pd.read_excel(url,
sheetname=0, header=1)

# View the first two rows
dataframe.head(2)
```

	5	2015-01-01 00:00:00	0
0	5	2015-01-01 00:00:01	0

1   9   `2015-01-01 00:00:02`   0

The above solution is comparable to the solution for loading CSV files. The most significant difference is the additional parameter sheetname. That stipulates which sheet in the Excel file we want to load. Sheetname can accept strings bearing the name of the sheet and integers pointing to sheet positions (zero-indexed). If you're going to load multiple sheets, you should include them as a list. For instance, sheetname=[0,1,2, "Monthly Sales"] will return a dictionary of Pandas DataFrames with the 1st, 2nd and 3rd sheets and the sheet named Monthly Sales.

Loading JSON Files

This is done using the read_json command that converts JSON files into Pandas objects:

```
# Load library
import pandas as pd

# Create URL
url                                       =
'https://tinyurl.com/simulated_json'

# Load data
dataframe      =      pd.read_json(url,
orient='columns')

# View the first two rows
```

```
dataframe.head(2)

category
datetime
integer
0
0
2015-01-01 00:00:00
5
1
0
2015-01-01 00:00:01
5
```

Loading a JSON file into Pandas is similar to the above solutions. The only difference is the orient parameter, which indicates to Pandas how the loaded JSON file is structured. However, it takes some experimentation to figure out which argument—whether split, records, columns, values or index—is the right one. The json_normalize tool converts semi-structured JSON data into a pandas DataFrame. You can also view the json_normalize documentation for more information.

SQL Database Querying

To load data from a database using the structured query language (SQL), you can use pandas.read_sql_query:

```python
# Load libraries
import pandas as pd
from sqlalchemy import create_engine

# Create a connection to the
database
database_connection =
create_engine('sqlite:///sample.db')

# Load data
dataframe =
pd.read_sql_query('SELECT * FROM
data', database_connection)

# View first two rows
dataframe.head(2)
```

	first_name	last_name	age	preTestScore	postTestScore
0	Jason	Miller	42	4	25
1	Molly	Jacobson	52	24	94

Of the solutions presented above, this one is applied to real-world datasets most. SQL is a language used for pulling data from databases. Here, you first use create_engine to create a connection to an SQL database engine known as SQLite. You then use pandas.read_sql_query to query the database and input the results into a DataFrame.

Data Wrangling

Data wrangling is a term used to describe the process of converting raw data into clean, organized formats that are ready for use. It converts and maps raw data into forms that can be used for tasks such as data analysis or machine learning. It is a very critical step in feature preprocessing where raw data is converted into other formats using algorithms or parsed into predefined data structures and deposited into a data sink for storage and future use. The most well-known structure used to wrangle data is the data frame, which is incredibly versatile. Often in tabular form, data frames appear like tables you would typically see in spreadsheets. Here is an example of a data frame built from data of passengers on a cruise ship named the Nautica:

```
# Load library
import pandas as pd

# Create URL
url = 'https://tinyurl.com/nautica-csv'

# Load data as a dataframe
dataframe = pd.read_csv(url)
```

```
# Show first 4 rows
dataframe.head(4)
Name                    PClass      Age
    Sex         Sexcode
0   Alen, Miss Elsa Walton 1st
        27.00       female      1
1   Alberto, Miss Helen Lori 1st
        5.00        female      1
2   Ally, Mr Hudson Josh 1st
        31.00       male        0
3   Ally, Mrs Hudgens 1st
        26.00       female      1
```

Important things to notice in this data frame:

1. Each row corresponds to an observation (i.e., a passenger) and every column corresponds to a feature such as age, sex, or passenger class.

2. Every column has a name, such as PClass or sex, and every row has an index number. These are used to select and manipulate observations and features.

3. The last two columns contain similar information in different formats. Because we want all of our features to be unique, we will have to eliminate one of them.

As we continue, we will examine several techniques that manipulate data frames using the Pandas library to create clean, well-structured observation sets for more preprocessing.

Data Frames

As mentioned before, data frames are the most common data structures used. By taking a deeper look at these structures—from how to create them to how you can view the data they contain, and more—we will be able to get a deeper understanding of how data is structured in machine learning systems. There are several methods to create a new data frame object using Pandas. One way is by using DataFrame to create an empty data frame and then define every column separately. For instance:

```python
# Load library
import pandas as pd

# Create DataFrame
dataframe = pd.DataFrame()

# Add columns
dataframe['Name'] = ['June Evans',
'Stephie Jenson']
dataframe['Age'] = [28, 25]
dataframe['Driver'] = [True, False]

# Show DataFrame
dataframe
```

```
      Name          Age Driver
0   June Evans       28    True
```

1   Stephie Jenson   25   False

Once the DataFrame object has been created, we can add new rows to the bottom:

```
# Create row
new_person    =    pd.Series(['Molly
Monroe,          50,            True],
index=['Name','Age','Driver'])

# Append row
dataframe.append(new_person,
ignore_index=True)
```

	Name	Age	Driver
0	June Evans	28	True
1	Stephie Jenson	25	False
2	Molly Monroe	50	True

While Pandas offers an infinite number of methods to create a DataFrame, creating an empty frame and then populating it with data seldom happens when using real-world data. Instead, these DataFrames are created from real data loaded from other sources such as a CSV, JSON file, or a database. You can also view some of the DataFrame's characteristics using Pandas commands such as dataframe.head to see the first few rows of the loaded dataset. Let's use the example from before of the passengers on the Nautica:

```
# Load library
import pandas as pd

# Create URL
url = 'https://tinyurl.com/nautica-
csv'

# Load data as a dataframe
dataframe = pd.read_csv(url)

# Show first 4 rows
dataframe.head(4)
```

| | Name | | PClass |
	Age	Sex	Sexcode
0	Alen, Miss Elsa Walton		1st
	27.00	female	1
1	Alberto, Miss Helen Lori		1st
	5.00	female	1
2	Ally, Mr Hudson Josh		1st
31.00		male	0
3	Ally, Mrs Hudgens		1st
	26.00	female	1

After running this code, the output will show the first four rows of the Nautica passenger data file. If you want to get descriptive statistics on any numeric column, you can use dataframe.describe:

```
# Show statistics
dataframe.describe()
```

	Age	SexCode
count	756	131
mean	30	0.352
std	14.	0.478
min	0.17	0
25%	21	0
50%	28	0
75%	39	0
max	71	1

After loading the data, it is important to understand the type of information contained in the file and how it is structured. You can choose to view the data directly. However, it can be difficult with real-world data because the files or databases can contain thousands to millions of rows and columns. Instead, we rely on viewing samples and calculating summary statistics based on the data.

In the example above, we are using a dataset for passengers on the Nautica from a particular voyage. Using dataframe.head, we can view the first few rows, usually five by default. We can also use dataframe.tail to view the last rows, dataframe.shape to see how many rows and columns the DataFrame contains, and dataframe.describe to display basic descriptive statistics of numerical column data. Note that sometimes the displayed statistics don't tell the full story. For instance, Pandas views the SexCode column as numeric because of the 1s and 0s. However, these values represent categories, thus the summary statistics don't make sense.

As you work with your data, you might be required to select individual data or slices of a dataframe. You can do this using the Pandas dataframe.loc or dataframe.iloc commands to select rows or values:

```
# Load library
import pandas as pd

# Create URL
url = 'https://tinyurl.com/nautica-csv'

# Load data as a dataframe
dataframe = pd.read_csv(url)

# Select first row
dataframe.iloc[0]

Name        Alen, Miss Elsa Walton
PClass      1st
Age         27
Sex         female
SexCode     1
Name: 0, dtype: object
```

We can use colons to define row slices we want, such as selecting the second and fourth rows:

```
# Select two rows
dataframe.iloc[1:4]
```

Name	PClass	Age	Sex	Sexcode
0	Alen, Miss Elsa Walton	1st		
	27.00	female	1	
3	Ally, Mrs Hudgens	1st		
	26.00	female	1	

DataFrames don't always require numerical indexing. This index can be set to any value, which is unique to each row. For instance, we can set the index to passenger names and pick rows using their name:

```
# Set index
dataframe                                    =
dataframe.set_index(dataframe['Name'
])
```

```
# Show row
dataframe.loc['  Alen,   Miss   Elsa
Walton']
```

Name	Alen, Miss Elsa Walton
PClass	1st
Age	27
Sex	female

```
SexCode    1
Name: Alen, Miss Elsa Walton, dtype:
object
```

Pandas contains a lot of commands that can help you when dealing with data, such as commands to help you select data conditionally, replace values, rename columns, and find unique or missing values. Others can delete a column or row, group rows, find the max, min, sum, mean, and the total count of a dataset, apply functions over column elements or groups, concatenate dataframes, merging them, and more.

Handling Different Data Types

The data used in machine learning systems can contain various types of data or features. These differing types of data require different feature preprocessing to make them usable in machine learning models. Common features include numerical features, categorical features, images, date and time, and text.

Feature Processing for Numerical Data

Quantitative data is a representation of measurement or count (e.g. age, monthly sales, salary paid, or class size) and is often represented numerically. Numerical data can be subcategorized into two groups: continuous data and discrete data.

From the examples above, the age of a person can be classified as discrete data, while their salary is an example of continuous data. To use numerical features effectively, we must process them using the following methods.

1. Normalization

Feature scaling is used to normalize the range between independent variables or data features. This process is referred to as normalization and it impacts non tree-based models more than tree-based ones. This means that if you want good results when using a non tree-based model, you should normalize your numerical data. There are several ways you can normalize features:

Rescaling, or Min-Max normalization: this is the simplest kind of normalization that rescales features to the range [0,1 or -1, 1]. It calculates using the following equation:

$$x'_i = \frac{x_i - \min(x)}{\max(x) - \min(x)}$$

Where x is the original feature value, and x'_I is the normalized value or the rescaled feature.

Here is a code snippet of Scikit-learn's MinMaxScaler command rescaling a feature:

```
# Load libraries

import numpy as np

from sklearn import preprocessing


# Create feature

feature = np.array([[-600.5],

                    [-110.1],

                    [0],

                    [150.1],

                    [800.9]])


# Create scaler

minmax_scale                            =
preprocessing.MinMaxScaler(feature_r
ange=(0, 1))


# Scale feature
```

```
scaled_feature                          =
minmax_scale.fit_transform(feature)
```

```
# Show feature
```

```
scaled_feature
```

```
array([[ 0.          ],
       [ 0.28671429],
       [ 0.35715286],
       [ 0.42957143],
       [ 1.          ]])
```

In this example, the outputted array displays feature rescaled between 0 and 1. Scikit-learn's MinMaxScaler has two options to rescale data. The first option is using fit_transform to compute the maximum and minimum values of a feature, them utilize the transform command to rescale the feature. The other option is to use the min_maxscale.fit_transform command to do these two actions at once. While there is no mathematical distinction between these two options, it can be beneficial to keep these operations apart because it lets you apply similar transformations to various datasets.

2. Standardization or Z-score normalization

This normalization scales a feature to be approximately standard normally distributed, such that its mean is zero and the variance is one. This is an alternative to the min-max scaling command discussed before. First, we use standardization to transform the data so that the mean ($\bar{x}$) is 0 and the standard deviation (σ) is 1. In this transformation, every element in the feature is transformed using the equation below:

$$x'_i = \frac{x_i - \bar{x}}{\sigma}$$

Where x'_1 is the standardized form of x_1. The transformed feature represents the number of standard deviations the original value is away from the mean of the feature. In statistics, this is referred to as z-score. This is a code snippet to illustrate standardizing a feature:

```
# Load libraries

import numpy as np

from sklearn import preprocessing
```

```python
# Create feature
x = np.array([[-1000.1],
              [-200.2],
              [500.5],
              [600.6],
              [9000.9]])


# Create scaler
scaler =
preprocessing.StandardScaler()


# Transform the feature
standardized =
scaler.fit_transform(x)


# Show feature
standardized


array([[-0.76058269],
```

```
[-0.54177196],

[-0.35009716],

[-0.32271504],

[ 1.97516685]])
```

Standardization is usually the go-to scaling technique used for preprocessing ML data, and it is utilized more than min-max scaling. However, this all depends on the learning algorithm used. Principal component analysis, for instance, usually works excellently using standardization while min-max is often favored for use in neural networks. Generally, its recommended to standardize features unless you have a particular reason to use the alternative.

Outlier Removal

An outlier is described as an observation point that is far from other observations. By removing outliers, you can significantly enhance the ML model's learning performance. If data contains significant outliers, it can have a negative impact on the standardization process, thus affecting the feature's mean and variance. This is especially true for non tree-based models. Tree-based models are robust to outliers.

Other feature preprocessing tasks include normalizing observations, generating polynomial and interaction features, transforming features, detection and removal of outliers, discretization features, deleting observations with missing values, imputing missing values, and so on.

Feature Preprocessing For Categorical and Ordinal features

Not all data can be quantitative. Objects can also be measured by their qualities. It is represented as an observation's membership to a discrete category such as brand, color, gender, etc. Categorical features have only limited and fixed possible values. For instance, if you have a dataset with info on users, you will find features like age or gender. Alternatively, with data on products, you will get features like product type, seller, manufacturer, etc. Categorical data features can be either nominal or ordinal. Nominal data includes information with no intrinsic order, such as colors or gender. Ordinal data, on the other hand, has some form of natural order, such as age or levels. Categorical data can also have continuous features, which are numerical variables that have an infinite number of values. These values can be numeric or date/time.

Despite what the data is used for, the major challenge with determining how to use this data in any ML model is hampered by the following constraints:

- Categorical features can have a lot of levels, referred to as high cardinality (e.g. locations or URLs), where many of the levels show up in a relatively small number of cases.

- Many ML models, such as regression or SVM, are algebraic. Thus, their data input must be numerical. To use these types of models, categories must be transformed into numerical form before applying the learning algorithm to them.

- While some machine learning packages or libraries can automatically transform categorical data to numerals based on a default embedding method, most ML packages don't support such inputs.

- For a computer, categorical data doesn't have the same context or information that humans can easily identify and understand. As an example, we've created a feature called "country" using data from three countries: Ghana, Senegal, and Italy. We can infer that Ghana is closely related to Senegal (as they are from the same continent) while Italy and Ghana are very different from each other (both in terms of location and culture). The model, however, views all three countries as three different levels (possible values) of the same feature country. Without the additional contextual information, the model cannot differentiate between the levels.

The challenge we face next is determining how to change these values into numeric form for further processing, and thus help us discover any hidden information this data may contain. The use of categorical data involves transforming it into numeric labels and applying some form of encoding to them. These encoding methods include:

- One Hot Encoding
- Label Encoding
- Ordinal Encoding
- Helmert Encoding
- Binary Encoding
- Frequency Encoding
- Mean Encoding
- Weight of Evidence Encoding
- Probability Ratio Encoding
- Hashing Encoding
- Backward Difference Encoding
- Leave One Out Encoding
- James-Stein Encoding
- M-estimator Encoding

It is important to understand that not all encoding will work for every ML model. You will need to search through trial and error to figure out which one works best for your model.

Chapter Summary

- Data is the lifeblood of machine learning. Therefore, the handling of data is crucial to the success of your ML model.
- There are different types of data used in ML models, namely numeric, categorical, date/time, text, images.
- How to handle numeric data, since most machine learning models prefer numeric input.
- How to create simulated datasets and how to load various data files into our ML systems.
- Looked at code snippets illustrating various functions used in the preprocessing of data.

Exercises

1. Using the DataFrame function, create and display a dataframe for the following data:
   a. Justin Maverick, age: 32, tall
   b. Phylis Winters, age: 26, short
   c. Florence Weathers, age: 39, tall
   d. Janice Ramirez, age: 55, short
2. Once you have created the new dataframe, add the following rows:
   a. Juan Pedro. age: 17, tall
   b. Franchesca Romanov, age: 44, short.
3. Once you are done, use the describe function to display the data's statistics.

4. Download the titanic dataset and apply the feature processing function we have looked at in this chapter.

Chapter Three:
Classification

Classification can be described as the process of predicting the class of given data points. Classes can sometimes be referred to as targets, labels, or categories. Classification Predictive Modeling is the process of approximating a mapping function (f) from inputted variables (x) to discrete outputted variables (y). Spam detection, for instance, is an example of a classification problem. Since there are only two classes, spam emails and non-spam emails, it is referred to as a binary classification.

A classifier uses training data to discern how given input parameters relate to the given class. In this case, known spam and non-spam emails are both utilized as training data. When the classifier is trained well, it can then be used to detect whether or not a new email is spam. We can also use data for when a customer applies for a bank loan. They are classified as either safe or risky depending on their age and salary. Classification falls under supervised learning, where the labels are also provided with the input data. There are several uses for classification in today's world, such as credit approval, target marketing, medical diagnosis, and more.

There are two types of classification learners: lazy learners and eager learners. Lazy learners store the training data and wait for testing data to appear. When it does, classification is carried out based on the most relevant data in the stored training dataset. Lazy learners spend more time predicting than training. Examples of lazy learners include k-nearest neighbor and case-based reasoning.

Eager learners, on the other hand, build classification models based on the given training dataset before retrieving data for classification. These learners must be able to commit to a single hypothesis that covers the whole instance space. Because of the model construction, these learners spend more time training than predicting. Examples of eager learners include decision trees, naive Bayes, artificial neural networks, etc.

Classification vs. Clustering

Classification and clustering are both learning methods that group objects using one or more features. They appear to be similar, but differ in the context of data mining. The main difference between the two is that classification is employed in supervised learning where predefined labels are given to feature instances. While clustering is used in unsupervised learning where similar instances are grouped based on their properties. These groups are known as clusters.

Here are some basic terminologies used in classification:

- Classifier - an algorithm used to map inputted data into a particular category.
- Feature - a singular measurable property of data being observed.
- Classification Model - used to predict the class, label, or category of new test data according to the results of the training data.
- Binary Classification - a classification task that has two possible outcomes (e.g. yes or no).
- Multi-class Classification - this task has more than two classes but only one label (e.g. a particular animal can be a cow or a goat, but not both).
- Multi-label Classification - this task maps samples to a set of target labels, and it has more than one class. For instance, an article can be about sports, fashion, a place, or a person all at the same time.

Classification Algorithms

There are several classification algorithms available, and it's difficult to say which one is superior to the other. As is the case with the other algorithms we've covered, it all depends on your application of it and the dataset used. For instance, if the dataset is linear, then a linear classifier (such as logic regression or Naïve Bayes classifiers) can perform better than other sophisticated models and vice versa. Classification Algorithms could be broadly classified as the following:

I.   Linear Classifiers
     A. Logistic regression
     B. Naive Bayes classifier
     C. Fisher's linear discriminant
II. Support vector machines
     A. Least squares support vector machines
III. Quadratic classifiers
IV. Kernel estimation
     A. k-nearest neighbor
V.   Decision trees
     A. Random forests
VI. Neural networks
VII. Learning vector quantization

Linear Classifiers

A linear classifier can be defined as a function that makes classification decisions based on the value of a linear combination of attributes. These attributes are also known as feature values, and they are presented to the computer as feature vectors. These types of classifiers work well for problems with many features, such as classifying documents by achieving high accuracy levels compared to non-linear algorithms.

Let's take a look at some linear classification algorithms:

- Logistic Regression

This classifier estimates discrete values (such as yes/no, alive/dead, 0/1, etc.) based on a given set of independent variables. It simply predicts an event's probability of occurring by fitting the data to a logit function, thus the name logit regression. The results will always lie between 0 and 1, since it foretells probability. Despite its namesake of "regression", it is important to remember that logistic regression is a classification algorithm, not a regression one.

Let us say, for instance, that you have an equation on a math test and it can only have two results. Either you solve it, or you don't. Now, if you are given several different equations to test what chapters you understood well, the outcome would be as follows:

1. If the problem is trigonometry based, you have a 70 percent chance of solving it.
2. If the problem is arithmetic, you have a 30 percent chance of solving it.

This is what logistic regression will give you. It calculates the odds of an outcome and models the log as a linear combination of the values used. The equation used looks like this:

```
odds=  p/  (1-p)  =  probability  of
event  occurrence  /  probability  of
event  occurrence  ln(odds)  =  ln(p/(1-
```

```
p))   logit(p)   =   ln(p/(1-p))   =
b0+b1X1+b2X2+b3X3....+bkXk)
```

Here, p is the probability of our desired feature's presence. The classifier selects the parameters that boost the chances of seeing the sample values instead of reducing the sum of squared errors like in an ordinary regression algorithm.

- Naive Bayes Classifier

This is a probabilistic classifier based on Bayes' theorem, under the assumption that the attributes are conditionally independent. It assumes that the presence of a certain feature in a class is unrelated to the presence of other features. Constructing a Bayesian model is quite simple, and it is especially useful when handling large datasets. Along with its simplicity, this classifier is known to perform better than sophisticated classification algorithms. Bayes' theorem calculates posterior probability $P(c|x)$ from $P(c)$, $P(x)$ and $P(x|c)$. The equation is as follows:

$$P(c|x) = \frac{P(x|c)P(c)}{P(x)}$$

Likelihood · Class Prior Probability · Posterior Probability · Predictor Prior Probability

$$P(c|X) = P(x_1|c) \times P(x_2|c) \times \cdots \times P(x_n|c) \times P(c)$$

Here, $P(c|x)$ represents the posterior probability of the target class with a given predictor (attribute). $P(c)$ represents the prior class probability. $P(x|c)$ represents the likelihood, which is the probability of predictor given class. $P(x)$ is the prior probability of a given predictor.

The classification is done by deriving the maximum posterior $P(c|X)$ with the above assumption applying to the theorem. The assumption greatly decreases the computational cost by counting the class distribution only. Even though this assumption might not be valid in most cases because the attributes are dependent, this classifier has performed well.

The Naïve Bayes classification algorithm is easily implemented, and it produces great results in most cases. It is also scalable, so it can handle large datasets since it takes linear time instead of using iterative approximation used by other classifiers.

There is, however, a downside to this classification. It is susceptible to a problem known as zero probability. When a particular attribute's probability is zero, it can fail to give a valid prediction. This can be solved using a Laplacian estimator.

Here's an example to better illustrate how this classifier works. Here, we have a training dataset of weather conditions, namely, rainy, overcast or sunny and a corresponding binary parameter, play. We need to classify whether kids can play or not based on how the weather is.

Weather	Play
Sunny	No
Overcast	Yes
Rainy	Yes
Sunny	Yes
Sunny	Yes
Overcast	Yes
Rainy	No
Rainy	No
Sunny	Yes
Rainy	Yes
Sunny	No
Overcast	Yes
Overcast	Yes
Rainy	No

Frequency Table

Weather	No	Yes
Overcast		4
Rainy	3	2
Sunny	2	3
Totals	5	9

Likelihood Table

Weather	No	Yes	
Overcast		4	4/14 = 0.29
Rainy	3	2	5/14 = 0.36
Sunny	2	3	5/14 = 0.36
Totals	5	9	
	5/14 = 0.36	9/14 = 0.64	

First, we will convert the dataset into a frequency table and create a likelihood table by finding the probabilities. For example, overcast probability = 0.29 and playing probability is 0.64. Now, using the Naïve Bayesian equation, we can calculate each class's posterior probability. The class with the greatest probability will be the prediction outcome. In this case, if we wanted to know whether or not the kids will play when it is sunny, we could solve it using the above equation:

P(Yes | Sunny) = P(Sunny | Yes) * P(Yes) / P (Sunny).

Here P (Sunny |Yes) = 3/9 = 0.33, P(Sunny) = 5/14 = 0.36, P(Yes)= 9/14 = 0.64. So P (Yes | Sunny) = 0.33 * 0.64 / 0.36 = 0.60, which has higher probability. So, according to the date, the kids will play when it is sunny. This is how the Naive Bayes classifier works. It is mostly used for text classification and for multi-class classification problems too.

Support Vector Machines

Support vector machines (SVM) are a kind of supervised ML algorithm which is used for classification and regression problems. Even though they are utilized for both classification and regression, they are mainly used in tackling classification problems. An SVM algorithm is performed by plotting every acquired data value as a point in n-dimensional space. Here "n" represents the total number of data features present. The value of each parameter is displayed as a particular coordinate. After distributing coordinate data, we can now classify it by finding the line or hyper-plane that distinctly divides and differentiates between the two data classes.

SVMs are kernel-based algorithms best used to separate two classes. A kernel refers to a computer function that converts the inputted data into a high dimensional space where the question or problem can be solved. Kernel functions are a type of algorithm class used for pattern analysis, and they can be either linear or nonlinear. The kernel's primary function is to get input data and transform it into the required output form. SVMs have several real-world applications, from image recognition to face detection, and even handwriting analysis.

Artificial Neural Networks

Artificial neural networks are a set of connected input and output units where each connection has a weight linked with it. It was started by psychologists and neurobiologists to make and test computational neuron analogs. As they learn, these networks adjust the weights so that they can predict the right class labels on the inputted data. Several neural networks have been developed for classification, such as feed-forward, recurrent, convolutional, etc. Selecting the right neural architecture depends on the model application. In most cases, feed-forward models give fairly accurate results, but convolutional networks perform better for image processing applications.

Depending on the complexity of the function to be mapped by the model, there can be many hidden layers in it. More hidden layers enable a model to map complex relationships, such as deep neural networks. However, this also means that it takes more time to train and adjust weights. This also results in poor model interpretability compared to other algorithms

due to the unknown symbolic meaning references by
the learned weights. These algorithms have performed
impressively in most real-world uses thanks to its high
noise tolerance and the ability to classify untrained
patterns. We will take a more extensive look at Neural
networks later in this book.

K-nearest Neighbor

The k-nearest neighbor algorithm is an example
of a lazy learner. This is because it stores all available
instances corresponding to training parameter points
in n-dimensional space. When a new parameter is
inputted, it analyzes the closest k-nearest neighbors
and returns the most common class as the prediction.
For real-valued data, it outputs the mean of the k-
nearest neighbors as the prediction. In the distance-
weighted function, it checks the contributions of each
of the k neighbors as per their distance using the
following query, giving greater weight to the closest
neighbors.

$$w \equiv \frac{1}{d(x_q, x_i)^2}$$

This algorithm is robust to noisy data, since it
averages the k-nearest neighbors.

Training a Binary Classifier

We will now take a look at training a binary classifier. As we mentioned before, a binary classifier can distinguish between two classes. To better understand this process, we will be using the MNIST dataset in our examples. This dataset contains about 70,000 images of handwritten numbers. You can download this dataset using Scikit-learn's fetch_mldata. By default, Scikit-learn stores all downloaded datasets in the $HOME/scikit_learn_data directory. Here is the function's code:

```
>>> from sklearn. datasets import
fetch_mldata

>>> mnist = fetch_mldata('MNIST
original')

>>> mnist

{'COL_NAMES': ['label', 'data'],

'DESCR': 'mldata.org dataset: mnist-
original',

'data': array([[0, 0, 0, ..., 0, 0,
0],

      [0, 0, 0, ..., 0, 0, 0],

      [0, 0, 0, ..., 0, 0, 0],
```

```
    ...,

    [0, 0, 0, ..., 0, 0, 0],

    [0, 0, 0, ..., 0, 0, 0],

    [0, 0, 0, ..., 0, 0, 0]],
dtype=uint8),
```

```
'target': array([ 0., 0., 0., ...,
9., 9., 9.])}
```

Let's say we want to identify one digit, the number 3. We want our binary classifier to be able to tell which images are 3 and which are not (-3). To start, we will create target vectors for the classification task at hand:

```
y_train_3 = (y_train == 3) # True
for all 3s, False for all other
digits.
```

```
y_test_3 = (y_test == 3)
```

Next, we will select a classifier such as a Stochastic Gradient Descent (SGD) classifier using Scikit-learn's SGDClassifier class and train it. This classifier is ideal because it can handle large datasets efficiently by handling training instances independently. This is why it is also used for online learning. It is important to note that during training, the SGDClassifier relies on randomness, thus the name stochastic. For reproducible results, set the random_state parameter. Below is a code snippet creating an SGDClassifier and training it:

```
from     sklearn.linear_model     import
SGDClassifier

sgd_clf                                    =
SGDClassifier(random_state=44)

sgd_clf.fit(X_train, y_train_3)
```

Now you can use it to identify images of the number 3:

```
>>> sgd_clf.predict([some_digit])

array([ True], dtype=bool)
```

The SGDClassifier guesses that this image represents a 3 (True). In this case, it was right. Now, we will evaluate its performance.

Evaluating a Classifier

Evaluating a classifier is a lot harder than evaluating a regression algorithm since there are a lot more performance measures to consider. After training the model, the most crucial part is assessing the classifier to verify its applicability.

Using Cross-Validation to Measure Model Accuracy

Over-fitting is a common problem in ML systems, and it can occur in most models. You can use k-fold cross-validation to verify that your model is not over-fitted. With this method, the dataset is randomly divided into k mutually-exclusive subsets by cross_val_score(), approximately equal in size. One is kept for testing while others are used for training. This process is repeated with each of the k folds.

While implementing cross-validation, you will occasionally need more control over the validation process than what cross_val_score() and similar functions provide. In such cases, you can implement cross-validation yourself, since the process is quite straightforward. The following function, StratifiedKFold, does roughly the same thing as cross_val_score()code. The StratifiedKFold class is a variation of KFolds that returns stratified folds made by preserving the percentage of samples for each class. With each iteration, the code clones the classifier, trains it on the training folds, and makes predictions on the test fold. It then counts the number of predictions that are correct and outputs their ratio.

Here is an illustration of how StratifiedKFold works:

```python
from sklearn.model_selection import
StratifiedKFold

from sklearn.base import clone


skfolds = StratifiedKFold(n_splits=3,
random_state=44)


for train_index, test_index in
skfolds.split(X_train, y_train_3):

    clone_clf = clone(sgd_clf)

    X_train_folds =
X_train[train_index]

    y_train_folds =
(y_train_3[train_index])

    X_test_fold = X_train[test_index]

    y_test_fold =
(y_train_3[test_index])


    clone_clf.fit(X_train_folds,
y_train_folds)

    y_pred =
clone_clf.predict(X_test_fold)
```

```
    n_correct = sum(y_pred ==
y_test_fold)

    print(n_correct  /  len(y_pred))  #
prints 0.9602, 0.9555 and 0.9495
```

When using the SGD classifier, sometimes the training and test dataset sizes differ in each fold, with a variance of, at most, ``n_classes``.

Now, let us use cross_val_score() to evaluate the SGDClassifier model using cross-validation with three folds. This means dividing the data into three, then making predictions and evaluating them on every fold using a system trained on the remaining folds. The cross_val_score() function will return a high accuracy prediction. However, since the model only has to tell if an image is a 3 or not, its accuracy will be high. This is why accuracy is not used as a performance measure, particularly when dealing with skewed datasets. This type of data contains classes that are more frequent than others.

Other performance measures include:

- Precision and Recall

In classification, precision is defined as the ratio of relevant instances among the outputted instances, while recall is the ratio of relevant feature instances that have been recovered over the total number of relevant instances. They are used as a measurement of relevance.

- Confusion Matrix

The idea behind this is to count the number of times instances of class X have been classified as class Y. For instance, you might want to know how many times the SGDClassifier got the images of 3s and 5s mixed up. To calculate the confusion matrix, you need a set of predictions to be compared to the actual targets first.

- ROC Curve (Receiver Operating Characteristics)

ROC curve is often used for visual comparison of classification algorithms, and it shows the trade-off between the true positive rate (also called sensitivity, recall, or detection probability) and the false positive rate (specificity). The area under the ROC curve is a measure of the accuracy of the model. When a model is closer to the diagonal, it is less accurate, and the model with perfect accuracy will have an area of 1.0.

Multi-class Classification

Multi-class classifiers, or multinomial classifiers, can distinguish between more than two classes. These include Random forest or Naïve Bayes' algorithms. Others, such as SVM or Linear classifiers, are strictly binary. Alternatively, you can use several binary classifiers to perform multi-class classification. For instance, you can make a system that classifies digits into 5 classes (0 to 4) by training 5 binary classifiers for every digit. When classifying an image, every classifier has to make a prediction for it and the result is the class whose classifier has the highest output. This is known as the One-versus-All (OvA) strategy.

You could also train a binary classification algorithm for every digit pair—one to differentiate 0s and 1s, another for 0s and 2s and so on. This is referred to as the One-versus-One (OvO) strategy. For N classes, you need to train N x (N-1)/2 classifiers. If you applied this to the MNIST dataset, you would have to create 45 binary classification algorithms. You would have to run any image you wanted to classify through each algorithm to see which one wins the most comparisons. OvO's main advantage is that every classifier only needs to be trained on the part of the dataset for the two classes that needs to be distinguished.

Some classifiers, like SVM, scale poorly with large datasets. With these types of algorithms, OvO is preferred since it is easier to train many classifiers on small-sized datasets than training fewer classifiers on larger datasets. However, OvA is preferred when using binary classifiers. When you try using a binary classifier for multi-class classification, Scikit-learn automatically runs OvA, as shown below:

```
>>> sgd_clf.fit(X_train, y_train) #
y_train, not y_train_3

>>> sgd_clf.predict([some_digit])

array([ 3.])
```

This code trains the SGDClassifier function on the training dataset using the original target classes from 0 to 4 (y_train) rather than the three-versus-all target classes (y_train_5). It then makes a prediction which, in this case, was the right one. But behind the scenes, Scikit-learn actually trained five binary classification algorithms, got their predictions, and selected the one with the highest score. To check the data within Scikit-learn, you can use the decision_function() method. Rather than giving once score per instance, it brings up five scores, one per class.

If you wanted to force Scikit-learn to use OvO or an OvA, you could use OneVsOneClassifier or OneVsRestClassifier classes. Simply make an instance and run the binary classifier to its maker. For instance, this code creates a multi-class classification algorithm using the one-versus-one strategy, based on an SGDClassifier:

```
>>> from sklearn.multiclass import
OneVsOneClassifier

>>>                ovo_clf              =
OneVsOneClassifier(SGDClassifier(ran
dom_state=44))

>>> ovo_clf.fit(X_train, y_train)

>>> ovo_clf.predict([some_digit])

array([ 3.])

>>> len(ovo_clf.estimators_)

45
```

If you used a random forest classifier, Scikit-learn won't use OvO or OvA because these classifiers can classify data instances into multiple classes directly. The prediction probability of this classifier is quite high, but to get even higher accuracy, you need to scale your data.

Multi-label Classification

Up to this point, in all the classification examples we have looked at, every instance has always been assigned to a single class. However, you might want your classifier to output several classes for each feature. If we take facial recognition, for instance, what should the classifier do if it identifies several people in one picture and it can only attach a single label per person recognized? If it was trained to identify three people (Alex, John, and Sarah) and it was shown a picture of Sarah and John, the model should output [0,1,1]—meaning Alex = no, John = yes, and Sarah = yes. A classification system that outputs multiple binary labels is referred to as a multi-label classification system. When evaluating a multi-label classifier, picking the right performance metric is key, and that depends on your project.

Multi-output Classification

This classification task, also referred to as multi-label-multi-output classification, generalizes multi-label classification where every label can be a multi-class with two or more possible values. To better illustrate this, let us create a model that eliminates noise from images. We input a noisy image, and the model should output a clean image that's represented as a pixel intensity array. The output will be multi-label, which is a single label per pixel, and every label can have multiple values as pixel intensity ranges from 0 to 255. So, a pixel can be clean with a pixel intensity of 72.

Error Analysis

Assuming that you have identified a model for your ML project, you will want to find ways to improve it. One way is by examining the errors your model makes when running prediction results. The first step in error analysis is taking a look at the confusion matrix. It will tell you how many times a classifier classified a feature incorrectly. By dividing each value in the confusion matrix by the number of features in the related class, you can compare error rates rather than looking at the number of errors the classifier made.

Examining the confusion matrix allows you to see the different ways you can enhance your model. It helps pinpoint where you should be focusing your efforts. For instance, if a classifier is used to distinguish which images are 3s are those that are not and the confusion matrix shows that most images of 3s are misclassified as 5s, you should work on fixing this particular confusion. You can gather more training data or develop new features to help the classifier distinguish 3s from 5s, such as an algorithm to count the number of loops in the image (i.e., 3 has two half loops while 5 has one). You could even preprocess the data to make features like half loops stand out more.

Chapter Summary

- We defined classification as the process of predicting the class of given values.
- We looked at the difference between classification and clustering.

- We examined a few terminologies used in relation to classification, such as binary classification, multi-class classification, and multi-label classification.
  - There are several classification algorithms you can use, such as decision trees, logistic regression, KNN, and so on.
  - These classifiers can be used for binary, multi-class, or multi-label classification of features.
- How to train a binary classifier and how to evaluate it and the various performance measures used to gauge how a model performs.
- How classifiers can assign multiple class labels to data or multiple outputs.
- Classification algorithms can be used in spam detection, in medical diagnosis such as in tumor cells detection, classification of drugs, and so on.

Exercises

Here are some practice exercises to help you enhance what you have learned so far.

1. Try to create a classification algorithm for the MNIST dataset that attains over 97% accuracy on the test dataset.

a. Tip: The K-NearestNeighborClassifier performs quite well in this task. All you need to do is to find good parameter values by running a grid search on the weights and n-neighbor parameters.

2. Write a function that moves an MNIST image in a particular direction, either left, right, up or down by two pixels. Then, create four copies (one per direction) for every image in the training set and add them to the training dataset. Finally, train your best ML model on this new, larger training set and gauge its accuracy on the test set.

   a. You will notice that your model performs even better now. This method of artificially expanding the training dataset is known as data augmentation or training set expansion. The shift() function from the scipy.ndimage.interpolation module works very well here. For instance, shift(image, [1, 3], cval=0) shifts the image 1 pixel down and 3 pixels to the right.

3. If you want to take on something more challenging, you can create a spam classifier. You need to download spam and non-spam or ham examples from the Apache SpamAssassin's public datasets. Unzip them

and take a look at how the data is formatted. Once you are done, divide the dataset into a training and a test set. Then try out different classification algorithms and if you can create an awesome spam classifier, with both high precision and recall.

Chapter Four:
Training Models

So far, we have treated ML models as singularities. From previous examples, you have seen how you can do a lot without knowing what goes on behind the scenes. You have learned to do things like train and evaluate a classifier, preprocess data so that it can give you the most accurate data and show underlying patterns, all without knowing how the model actually got all this done. Just like with any software implementation, many times, you don't need to know what's going on.

Nevertheless, it is good to have a basic understanding of how things work, that way you can pick the most suitable model for your project faster, select the best parameters for your task, and choose the right training algorithms to use. It can also help you debug your system in case something goes wrong and perform more effective error analysis. The topics we will look at in this chapter will be vital in understanding, creating, and training neural networks, which we will look at later.

We will use a linear regression model—since it is a fairly simple model—and discuss two ways it can be trained. The first way is by using a direct, closed-form equation that computes the system parameters that best suit the system to the training dataset directly.

That is, it calculates the model parameters that reduce the cost function over the training set. The second method utilizes a repetitive optimization approach called gradient descent (GD). It changes the model parameters to reduce the cost function over the training dataset, which eventually converges to the same parameters as the first method.

We will then examine polynomial regression, which is a more sophisticated algorithm model that can be used to process nonlinear datasets. This model is more prone to overfitting since there are more parameters. We will have to look at ways of detecting whether or not the data was over-fitted by using learning curves and regularization methods to reduce the risk of over-fitting.

This chapter will contain a lot of mathematical equations that use the basic principles of linear algebra and calculus. To grasp these equations, you must know what vectors and matrices are, what transposing them entails, what dot product and matrix inverse is, and what partial derivatives are. Please go through linear algebra and calculus tutorials if you are unfamiliar with these concepts or if you need a refresher course. You can still understand what this chapter is all about without having to wholly get these linear algebra and calculus concepts, but brushing up on it couldn't hurt.

Linear Regression

A linear regression algorithm is a model that predicts the outcome by calculating the weighted sum of the input data plus the bias term. This bias term is a constant value, also referred to as the intercept term. A linear regression algorithm equation is as follows:

$$\hat{y} = \theta_0 + \theta_1 x_1 + \theta_2 x_2 + \cdots + \theta_n x_n$$

Where $\hat{y}$ is the prediction output, n is the number of features, x_1 is the ith feature value, and θ_1 is the jth parameter of the model, which includes the bias term θ_0 and value weights θ_1 to θ_n. This equation can be written in a more concise vectorized form as illustrated below:

$$\hat{y} = h_\theta(\mathbf{x}) = \theta^T \cdot \mathbf{x}$$

Here, θ represents the model's parameter vector which contains the bias term θ_0 and feature weights θ_0 to θ_n. while θ^T is the transpose value of θ. The feature vector is represented by x, which contains x_0 to x_n and is always equal to 1. θ^T .x is the dot product of θ^T and x while h_θ is a hypothetical function derived using the model parameters θ.

Now that you know what a linear model is, we can move on to training it. Training a model requires us to set its variables to best fit the model to the training dataset. Thus, we need to measure how well or badly the algorithm fits the dataset. For regression models, the most commonly-used performance measure is Root Mean Square Error (RMSE). Therefore, if we want to train a linear regression algorithm, we have to find the θ value that decreases the RMSE most, and brings back the same result, since values that minimize functions also minimize the square root. The MSE of a linear regression hypothesis h_θ on a training dataset X is determined using the following equation:

$$\text{MSE}(\mathbf{X}, h_\theta) = \frac{1}{m} \sum_{i=1}^{m} \left(\theta^T \cdot \mathbf{x}^{(i)} - y^{(i)} \right)^2$$

m - the number of instances you are measuring the MSE on in a particular dataset. For example, if you want to calculate the MSE of a dataset with 400 variables, then m=400.

x(i) - the vector of all the parameter values except the label of the ith instance in the dataset, and y(i) is the label or desired output value for that instance.

X - the matrix that has all the feature values for all instances except the labels. There is a single row per instance, and the ith row is equal to the transpose of x(i), denoted as (x(i))T.6

h_θ - the model's prediction function, also known as a hypothesis which is parametrized by the vector θ. When your system is given an instance's feature vector x(i), it gives a predicted output value $\hat{y}(i)$ = h(x(i)) for that feature instance.

Note: lowercase font is used when denoting scalar values (such as m or y(i)) and function names (such as h), while lowercase bold font is used for vectors (such as x(i)), and uppercase bold font for matrices (such as X).

The Normal Equation

Normal equation (NE) is a technique used to compute the value of theta (θ) that reduces the cost function. This mathematical equation is also called the closed-form solution, and will give us the result directly. The normal equation is used to solve the OLS Regression problem because it can find coefficients analytically. Unlike Gradient Descent, it is a one-step learning algorithm. The normal equation looks like this:

$$\hat{\theta} = \left(\mathbf{X}^T \cdot \mathbf{X}\right)^{-1} \cdot \mathbf{X}^T \cdot \mathbf{y}$$

Where the result (theta hat) is the θ's value used to reduce the cost function, and y is the value of the target parameter containing y(1) to y(m).

Now, let's produce some linear data to test this equation out.

```
import numpy as np

X = 2 * np.random.rand(100, 1)

y = 4 + 3 * X + np.random.randn(100,
1)
```

As we calculate theta hat using the NE, we'll use the inv() function from np.linalg (NumPy's linear algebra module) to calculate the matrix inverse and the dot() matrix multiplication method.

```
X_b = np.c_[np.ones((100, 1)), X]  #
add x0 = 1 to each instance

theta_best                          =
np.linalg.inv(X_b.T.dot(X_b)).dot(X_
b.T).dot(y)
```

We used the $y = 4 + 3x_0 +$ Gaussian noise function to generate the data and this is what the equation found:

```
>>> theta_best

array([[ 4.2151],

       [ 2.7701]])
```

The outcome we wanted was for $\theta_0 = 4$ and $\theta_1 = 3$ instead of $\theta_0 = 3.865$ and $\theta_1 = 3.139$. This was because the noise in the data made it hard to get the exact results we hoped for. However, you can now make predictions based on your outcome:

```
>>> X_new = np.array([[0], [2]])

>>> X_new_b = np.c_[np.ones((2, 1)), X_new] # add x0 = 1 to each instance

>>>             y_predict             = X_new_b.dot(theta_best)

>>> y_predict

array([[ 4.2151],

        [ 9.7553]])
```

Normal Equation and Computational Complexities

When the features in a dataset get larger, the NE gets slow because it calculates the inverse of $X^T \cdot X$, which is an $n \times n$ matrix where n represents the number of features. Depending on the implementation, the computational complexity of such a matrix inversion is normally $O(n^{2.4})$ to $O(n^3)$. In simpler terms, if you were to triple the number of features, you would then multiply the computational time by around $3^{2.4} = 13.97$ to $3^3 = 27$.

On the plus side, this equation is linear in relation to the number of features in the training dataset(O(m)). So it can take on more massive datasets quite efficiently as long as they fit into the machine's memory. Additionally, once you have trained your linear regression system using NE or any other algorithm, it will be able to make predictions very quickly. Also, the computational complexity is linear in relation to the number of features and instances you want to make predictions on. This means making predictions on twice or three times as many instances or features will take twice or three times as much time.

Now we will look at the many ways we can train a linear regression model suited instances where there are a lot of features or too many instances to save to memory.

Gradient Descent

This is a generic optimization algorithm that can find optimal solutions to many ML problems. Ideally it changes and tweaks parameter repeatedly to minimize the cost function. Let's say you were lost on a hill in a dense forest. The best thing to do would be to find your way down the hill by following the direction of the steepest slope. This is what GD does: it calculates the error function's local gradient in relation to the parameter vector θ and goes in the direction of the decreasing gradient. Once it is at zero, you have reached the function's minimum. You can then begin filling theta with random values (random initialization) and gradually improve it as you try to decrease the cost function, for example, using MSE until the algorithm converges to a minimum.

In GD, the size of the steps taken to reduce the cost function is determined by the learning rate hyperparameter. If it is too small, the regression model will have to deal with repetition in the convergence, and this takes a longer time to process. Alternatively, if it is too high, you might miss the convergence and end up on the other side of the cost function, resulting in divergence with larger values; and thus, the algorithm will fail to find a good solution. Most real-world cost functions will have holes, ridges plateaus, and all kinds of irregular terrain. This makes minimum convergence quite hard. Take a look at the graph example below:

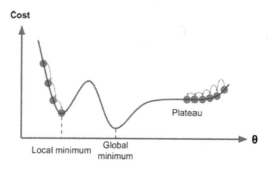

If the algorithm starts random initialization on the left, it will focalize to a local minimum, which isn't as good as the global minimum. If it instead starts on the right, then it will take a very long time to cross the irregular terrain; and if you stop the algorithm too early, you will never reach the global minimum convergence.

Luckily, the RMSE cost function for linear regression models is convex. So, if you select any two points on the curve, the line section that joins them never crosses the curve. What this means is that there are no local minimums, just one global minimum. It is also an endless function with a slope that doesn't change abruptly. Thus GD is guaranteed to get quite close to the global minimum—that is, if you wait long enough and if the algorithm's learning rate is not too high. When using GD, you have to ensure that all features have the same scale by using Scikit-learn's StandardScaler class, or it will take a lot longer to converge.

You should note that training a model means looking for the right model parameter combination that reduces a cost function. This is done by searching a model's parameter space. The more the model parameters, the more dimensions the space has, and this makes it harder to search for the right combination. Think of it this way: imagine searching for a needle in a 200-dimension haystack compared to a three dimensional one. Obviously, it is a lot trickier. Luckily, since the cost function is convex, the needle is at the bottom of the curved bowl.

Batch Gradient Descent

To execute GD, you have to calculate the gradient of the cost function in relation to every parameter of the model (θ_j). Simply put, you have to compute how changes in θ_j affect the cot function. This is referred to as a partial derivative. It's like asking what the slope of this hill is if I face west? Then, ask the same query for all the other directions or dimensions in the parameter space. The equation below calculates the partial derivative of the cost function in relation to the θ_j parameter denoted here as:

$$\frac{\partial}{\partial \theta_j} \text{MSE}(\theta) = \frac{2}{m} \sum_{i=1}^{m} \left(\theta^T \cdot \mathbf{x}^{(i)} - y^{(i)} \right) x_j^{(i)}$$

Rather than calculating this gradient one by one, you can compute them in one go using the following equation. Here the gradient vector, $\nabla_\theta \text{MSE}(\theta)$, has all the partial derivatives of the cost function. This formula, however, is very slow when handling large datasets because it involves calculations over the full training dataset X at every step, hence the name Batch Gradient Descent.

$$\nabla_\theta \text{MSE}(\theta) = \begin{pmatrix} \dfrac{\partial}{\partial \theta_0}\text{MSE}(\theta) \\ \dfrac{\partial}{\partial \theta_1}\text{MSE}(\theta) \\ \vdots \\ \dfrac{\partial}{\partial \theta_n}\text{MSE}(\theta) \end{pmatrix} = \dfrac{2}{m}\mathbf{X}^T \cdot (\mathbf{X} \cdot \theta - \mathbf{y})$$

Once you have your result, which points uphill, just start moving in the opposite direction to go down the hill. This means subtracting $\nabla_\theta \text{MSE}(\theta)$ from θ. This is also where the learning rate denoted as η comes in. To determine the size of the downhill step, you will multiply η by the gradient vector with the following equation:

$$\theta^{\text{next step}} = \theta - \eta \nabla_\theta \text{MSE}(\theta)$$

Here is a code snippet illustrating a quick implementation of this algorithm.

```
eta = 0.1 # learning rate

n_iterations = 1000

m = 100

theta = np.random.randn(2,1) #
random initialization

for iteration in range(n_iterations):
```

```
gradients = 2/m *
X_b.T.dot(X_b.dot(theta) - y)

theta = theta - eta * gradients
```

The resulting theta looks like this

```
>>> theta

array([[ 4.21509616],

       [ 2.77011339]])
```

This is exactly the same result as the normal equation found earlier, which means that the GD algorithm worked well. If we used different values for eta—0.05 and 0.5. for example—the equation would yield different results. The 0.05 learning rate would be too slow, and you might stop the algorithm before it gets to the solution. The inverse is true for the 0.5 learning rate eta. It will be too high, and the algorithm will jump the solution getting further and further away with each computation.

You can use a grid search to find a suitable learning rate, but you should limit the number of iterations so that the grid search eliminates slow models. So, how do you set the right number of iterations? You don't want to set it too low or too high. A simple solution would be to set a large number of repetitions and keep an eye on the algorithm. You want to stop it when the gradient vector becomes very small. This is because it has almost reached the minimum.

Stochastic Gradient Descent

Batch GD's biggest drawback is that it uses the whole dataset to compute the gradient at every step, and thus can be prolonged when handling large datasets. On the other hand, Stochastic Gradient Descent (SGD) randomly elects instances at every training step and calculates the gradients based on that singular instance. This makes the algorithm faster since it has less data feature to manipulate. SGD also makes training with more massive datasets possible, and it can be implemented as an out of core algorithm as well.

Due to its random nature, the SGD algorithm is less regular than batch GD, and thus decreases only on average. As time passes, it will get close to the minimum and produce a good result. However, since the data bounces around, it will never get us the optimal results we're looking for. This makes it ideal for irregular cost functions such as the example shown earlier because it escapes settling for the local minimum. And while randomness might be an excellent solution to avoiding the local minimum, it also means that the algorithm will never settle at the global minimum either.

The only way to solve this problem is by gradually reducing the learning rate. You start out with large steps, quickly escaping the local minimum, and then reduce them to help the algorithm settle at the global minimum. This process is referred to as simulated annealing, and the function that determines the learning rate at each repetition is known as the learning schedule. However, if the learning rate was reduced too fast, the algorithm could get stuck at the local minimum. Inversely, it would take too long getting to the minimum if it slowed too slowly, and you could end up with a suboptimal result.

When performing linear regression using SGD with Scikit-learn, you can use the SGDregressor function, which optimizes the squared error cost function. This code runs 50 epochs (an epoch is one complete round of iterations), beginning with a learning rate of 0.1 (eta0=0.1) using the set learning schedule without any regularization (penalty=None):

```
from     sklearn.linear_model     import
SGDRegressor

sgd_reg   =   SGDRegressor(n_iter=50,
penalty=None, eta0=0.1)

sgd_reg.fit(X, y.ravel())
```

Once again, the solution comes close to the one we got using the Normal Equation:

```
>>> sgd_reg.intercept_,
sgd_reg.coef_

(array([ 4.18380366]), array([
2.74205299]))
```

Mini-batch Gradient Descent

The final GD variant we will look at is Mini-batch Gradient Descent. Instead of calculating the gradient using the full dataset (BGD) or using just a single instance (SGD), it computes the gradients of small random sets of instances referred to as mini-batches. Its most significant advantage over SGD is that you get a performance boost from hardware optimization of matrix operations, especially when using graphic processing units. Its progress is less erratic compared to SGD's as it descends, and is therefore more likely to get a lot closer to the global minimum. However, escaping the local minimum is harder for Mini-batch GD. Thus, mini-batch GD makes a compromise between the fast convergence and the noise linked to gradient updates, which makes it a more flexible and robust algorithm.

Polynomial Regression

So far, we have looked at how we would process linear data, but what if the data you have was more complex? How would you process it? You could use a linear model and fit the non-linear data to it by adding the powers of each feature as new features and training a linear model on this extended dataset. This technique is referred to as polynomial regression.

To better understand how polynomial regression works, let's generate some random data by first using a quadratic equation $y=ax2+bx+c+$Gaussian noise:

```
m = 100

X = 6 * np.random.rand(m, 1) - 3

y = 0.5 * X**2 + X + 2 +
np.random.randn(m, 1)
```

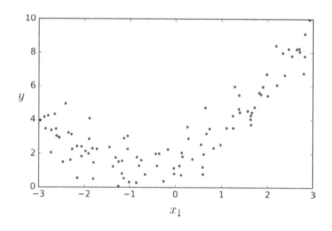

It is clear that a straight line will never fit the data properly, so we will use Scikit-learn's PolynomialFeatures class to change the data by adding the square (2nd degree polynomial) to every feature as new features. There is only one feature in our example:

```
>>> from sklearn.preprocessing
import PolynomialFeatures

>>> poly_features =
PolynomialFeatures(degree=2,
include_bias=False)

>>> X_poly =
poly_features.fit_transform(X)

>>> X[0]

array([-0.7528])

>>> X_poly[0]

array([-0.7528, 0.5666])
```

X_poly now has the original feature of X plus its square. Now you can fit a regression model to this expanded dataset:

```
>>> lin_reg = LinearRegression()

>>> lin_reg.fit(X_poly, y)
```

```
>>> lin_reg.intercept_,
lin_reg.coef_

(array([ 1.7814]), array([[ 0.9337,
0.5646]]))
```

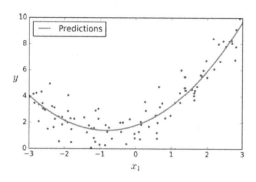

This is what the outcome from the extended dataset would look like. It estimates that $\hat{y} = 0.6x_1^2 + 0.9x_1 + 1.8$ when in fact the original function was $y = 0.5x_1^2 + 1.0x_1 + 2.0 + $ Gaussian noise. It is important to note that with multiple features, polynomial regression can find relationships between the features that linear regression models cannot. This is because the PolynomialFeatures class adds all feature combinations to a certain degree. For instance, if we had two features, d and g, PolynomialFeatures with a degree=3 would add not only the features d2, d3, g2, and g3, but also the combinations dg, d2g, and dg2.

Learning Curves

It stands to reason that if you performed high-degree polynomial regression, the training data would fit better than with a linear regression model. For instance, if we applied a 200-degree polynomial model to the data we generated in the previous example, it would fit more instances. However, this high-degree model is overfitting the data greatly, while the linear model underfits the data. So how do you decide how complex your regression model should be? And how can you tell if it is underfitting or overfitting the dataset?

In previous chapters, we looked at how cross-validation can be used to gauge a model's generalization performance. If it delivers well on the training data but poorly on the test data, then it is overfitting. If it performs poorly on both datasets, then it is underfitting. This is a simple way of telling if your model is too simple or complex. Alternatively, you can look to the learning curves. These are the plots of the model's performance on the training and validation datasets as a function of the training dataset size. To produce these plots, we have to severely train the model on various sized subsets of the training data.

If your model is underfitting the data, adding more training examples will not help. What you need to do is make either a more complex model or better features. With overfitting, however, more training data can help the validation error reach the training error.

The Bias/Variance Trade-off

In ML, a model's generalization error can be shown as the summation of three distinct errors:

- Bias - This refers to the error caused by the model's simple assumptions in fitting the data. A high-bias regression model is most likely to underfit the data.
- Variance - This refers to the error caused when a complex model tries to fit data. It occurs in part is as a result of the model's excessive sensitivity to small variations in the training data. A model with many degrees of freedom will have high variance, which results in overfitting.
- Irreducible error – This refers to the error caused in part by the noisiness of the data itself. Cleaning up the data can help reduce this error.

Making a model more complex will increase its variance and decrease its bias and vice versa. This is referred to as the bias/variance trade-off. Ideally, an ML model should have low variance and low bias. However, achieving this is practically impossible. So, in order to get a model that performs well on both the training and testing datasets, a trade-off has to be made.

Chapter Summary

We discussed the different ways we can train a machine learning model.

- We looked at linear regression, a simple model, prevalent in machine learning used to process linear data. On the other hand, polynomial regression models are used with non-linear datasets.

- We discussed two ways to train linear regression models, namely using the Normal Equation and Gradient Descent.

- While looking at the Normal Equation, we learned how it used to find the cost function coefficients analytically and give a direct result.

- Still, under normal equation, we also took a look at the computational problems that could arise while using the equation.

- Gradient descent is another way linear regression models are trained, and it has several variants, namely batch gradient descent, stochastic gradient descent, and mini-batch gradient descent.

- We then moved on to polynomial regression and what using them to train a machine learning model entails.
- With polynomial regression overfitting or underfitting the data can occur depending on the simplistic or complex nature of the model.
- We looked at ways to identify and fix this issue, such as using the PolynomialFeatures class to fit the data or learning curves.
- To get a perfectly working model, a trade-off between bias and variance has to occur.

Exercises

1. Name a linear regression training algorithm you could use if your training dataset contained millions of features?
2. Let's say that the features have very different scales. Which algorithms may suffer because of this, and how? Is there any way you can fix this?
3. Can GD get stuck in a local minimum when training a regression model?
4. Do all GD algorithms lead to the same model provided you let them run long enough?
5. Assume you are using Batch Gradient Descent and you are plotting the validation error at
6. every epoch. If you observe that the error is going up consistently, what do you suppose is happening, and how can you resolve it?

7. Is stopping Mini-batch GD when the validation error increases a good idea?

8. Among the Gradient Descent algorithms we discussed, which will get closest to the optimal solution the fastest? Which one among them will actually converge, and how can you get the others to converge too?

Chapter Five:
Model Evaluation and Selection

The world today is data-oriented, and more and more decisions are based on ML models. As such, we need to learn how to select the best models and also how to evaluate them. Machine learning libraries like Scikit-learn and Keras, have made it a lot easier to fit various machine learning models to a particular dataset. The challenge, therefore, becomes selecting the right model among the many that best suits your problem. You might think that having chosen a model that its performance is sufficient, but there are other factors to consider, such as how long it takes to train the model and ease of use. These factors matter because the model chosen could be used for months or even years. Take a credit card fraud detection system; for instance, the system must quickly learn to detect various fraud instances and bank employees must also know how to use the system else, what use is it to the bank.

Also, when selecting a model, you need to think about what you are choosing exactly. Are you just selecting an algorithm to fit the model or the whole data preparation and model fitting pipeline? After painstakingly selecting a model, you will want to assess its performance. After all, you took the time to select the model, so you want to be sure that it is working well. Fitting a model to our training data is one thing, but how can we be sure that it generalizes well to unlabeled and unclassified data? How can we tell that it didn't simply memorize the training data and might fail in making useful predictions on unseen data in the future? In this chapter, we will answer all these questions.

Model Selection

Model selection can be defined as the process of picking a final ML model from the final candidate list of models used on a training dataset. This process can also be applied when choosing between different algorithms (such as decision trees, logistic regression, etc.) and even when selecting different configurations of a particular model (such as different PCA algorithms). Suppose we have a dataset that we want to create a classification model for. We don't know which model will work best for this particular dataset because its unknowable. However, we can fit and assess different models and select the best one among them. This is basically what model selection is, and it is very different from model evaluation. When we evaluate potential models to choose the most appropriate one, this is model selection. Whereas model evaluation occurs once we have selected a model and want to test it out and see how well it will perform.

Considerations to Make When Selecting a Model

Fitting models is relatively easy; the real challenge of applied machine learning is selecting the best one among them. To do this, you have first to define what best means here. Understand that all models will have some predictive error due to the noise contained in the data, missing data values, and its limitations. Therefore, getting a perfect model is impossible; what you should look for instead is a model that comes close, one that is good enough.

When choosing a final model, the first step is finding one that fits the specific requirements you may have. For instance, you might be interested in choosing the best hyperparameters for the chosen model. Hyperparameters control the learning method's parameters, which are specified before training (such as in the k-nearest neighbor algorithm). In contrast, model parameters control how the input features will transform into the target output. Finding the optimal hyperparameters for a model is crucial to its performance on the given data. The learning method (and corresponding optimal hyperparameters) is another factor to consider. Therefore, a good model can be a lot of things, all of which are project-specific such as meeting your requirements and constraints or being skillful enough with the available time and

120

resources, when compared to other models, relative to the test data and its complexity.

Step two is considering what is being selected. What this means is that we are not selecting a fit because all models would be disqualified since we will fit the data to the final model. So, we are selecting the algorithms used to fit the data to the final model. Why does this matter, you ask? As seen in the previous chapter, some algorithms need the data they are processing to be prepared so that they can find the best solution to the ML problem. Thus our model selection process has an extra step where we choose model development pipelines.

These pipelines can take in the same training dataset and output models that can be assessed equally. Still, each model may require differing or overlapping computational steps such as filtering and transforming data or feature engineering and selection, etc. The closer you look at the selection, the more nuances you discover. The most important factors to keep in mind as you make your selection are:

- Is the model interpretable – is it easy to understand why the model make the decisions the way it does?
- The model's complexity – how easy the model is to explain and understand.
- The model's accuracy in making predictions.

- Its speed – in terms of learning and testing.
- Is the model scalable – can it be used on large datasets.

To get the right model, trade-offs among these qualities must be made. Now that you understand some of the considerations to make while selecting a model, let's look at selection methods.

In an ideal situation, the best approach to selecting a model would require you to have sufficient data that would be split into training, validation, and testing datasets. The training set would then be fit to potential models, evaluated, and selected using the validation sets, and finally, their performance would be tested using the testing data. Unfortunately, for most datasets, you will never have enough data, let alone be able to gauge what amount is sufficient for the specific problem.

Model Evaluation

Model evaluation is an essential part of any model development process. When selecting models, their performance plays a significant role, and we need to gauge it to get the best model. Evaluation helps you find the best model that represents your data and also assess how well the selected model will work in the future. The goal of model evaluation is estimating the generalization error of the model chosen; that is, how well it performs on unseen data. Needless to say, an excellent model will perform well in training and testing data. Hence the need to be sure that a model's performance will not diminish when processing new data.

The difference between model selection and evaluation is important because of overfitting. If we assess the model's generalization on the same data it was trained on; we will not get an accurate idea of how it will perform. This is because it already knows the relationships between the data features. You can use validation to help you get an unbiased estimate of a model's skill. Validation aims to help with algorithm selection, hyperparameter tuning, and it is used as a measure of a model's generalizability. In algorithm selection, validation strategies are used to select the most appropriate model classes for the data, such as whether to use neural nets, tree-based models, or linear models; in hyperparameter tuning, these techniques help in finding the optimal model hyperparameters to increase its predictive power. Lastly, validation is used to gauge a model's generalizability; this is how well the model can process unseen data. The first two objectives are classified under model selection because here, we select the model's algorithm and its optimal hyperparameters; the third objective deals with the model's assessment.

Model Evaluation Methods

With that in mind, let's take a look at different validation techniques. Validation techniques are used to compute a model's accuracy or error rate. Take, for instance, buying a highly reviewed product from amazon only for it to breakdown after a few uses. This is a classic case of things looking promising only for them to quickly collapse. Without proper model assessment and validation, you could launch a model that does not perform as advertised, the best-case scenario being you have wasted time because you have to retrain the model. Worse case, the model could cost you a lot of money or even endanger human lives (medical diagnosis models).

The first step in any validation process is splitting your data during training to understand what happens when the model is faced with data it hasn't seen before. The most prevalent splitting method is the Scikit-learn's train_test_split, which randomly splits the data so we can see how the model performs using unseen data from the same dataset. This is also called hold-out validation. Using this hold-out method does have one disadvantage; the data can be divided into a subset with different concentration of features since there most real-world data is never evenly distributed. This is referred to as the sampling bias, which is a systematic error that occurs due to a non-random data sample's feature population distribution that causes some features to be less likely to be included than others. Validation methods like k-validation can help combat sampling bias.

Hold-out Validation

As stated before, the data is randomly split into a training and test dataset. The training set is then split to create a validation set. A common training-validation set split ratio is 80:20. However, this is may not always be the case, as seen with time-series data. With this type of data, splitting should be done chronologically with the test data containing the most recent data because it is most similar to what the model will face in production. When using hold-out validation, the choice of test dataset size is a crucial one. If it is too large, then an underestimation of the model's predictive power might occur (the model will have a high bias), but the prediction will be more stable (low variance). An ideal model should have low bias and low variance balance. The test dataset should be about 20% of the whole dataset, so you have enough data to train the model. Don't use the same holdout set to perform both model selection and evaluation as the outcome will be positively biased.

Some of the upsides of this method are that validation data is entirely independent of the training dataset since it is separate from it. So our validation sample or the intermediate testing set is relatively pure. Here training and validation take place only once, making this process computationally cheap compared to cross-validation. It does, however, have disadvantages such as being prone to sampling bias and its inability to generalize well. What this means is that the error estimate in the validation set can be very high depending on the observations that were in the training set and those in the validation dataset.

Repeated hold-out validation (Monte Carlo cross-validation) - This approach enables you to get a better model performance estimate that is less dependent on the data splitting. It repeats the holdout method k times using different random datasets. The accuracy of the model will be the average performance of the model over k repetitions. The model is tested on more test samples than in the other hold-out method, and it helps reduce the prediction's variance. It is, however, more computationally expensive than single hold-out validation

Here is what repeated hold-out validation looks like:

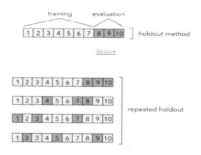

K-fold Cross-Validation

In chapter three, we talked briefly talked about cross-validation as a measure of a binary classifier's accuracy. This was an example of how cross-validation can be used in model assessment. Here we will delve deeper into k-fold cross-validation and its many variations. k-fold cross-validation (k-fold CV) is when the data is stochastically split into 'k' groups with one of the groups acting as the test dataset and the rest as training data and averages the results. This process is repeated until all k-groups have been used as test subjects. Take the following illustration, for instance. It shows a 5-fold cross-validation process.

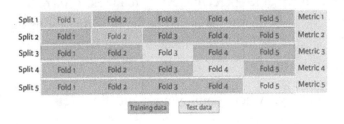

By using every dataset for training and testing, the chances of sampling bias occurring are significantly reduced. Ideally, k=10 is a good number of folds for k-fold cross-validation. Another benefit of this is that all observations get to be used for training and testing. The results of each fold can be quite insightful. Even though they are mostly used to calculate the model's average performance, by looking at the standard deviation between the results, you can tell a lot about the model's stability when using different data inputs.

When using k-fold CV, there are some important points to note. First, k-fold CV assumes that every observation was independently generated, i.e., the data is independent identically distributed, IID). If your data is IID, its best to shuffle observations when assigning folds, and you can use scikit-learn shuffle=True. Secondly, if you are using it to assess a classifier, your folds should roughly contain similar observation percentages from each target class (stratified k-fold). For instance, if your target vector had 70% red and 30% green, then each fold should have the same percentage of features (70 red-30 green). This feature balance can be obtained by using the StratifiedKFold class instead of the KFold class in Scikit-learn.

Finally, when employing validation sets, it is important to preprocess the data based on the training set and then apply those changes to both datasets. For example, when we fit our standardization object, standardizer, we compute the mean and standard variance of the training data only. Then we apply that transformation (using transform) to both the training and test sets. This is because we were assuming that the test data is unseen, and if we fit both our preprocessors using observations from both sets, some of the data from the test set leaks into our training set.

This rule applies to any preprocessing step, such as feature selection.

```
# Import library

from sklearn.model_selection import
train_test_split

# Create training and test sets

features_train,         features_test,
target_train,        target_test         =
train_test_split(

features,     target,     test_size=0.1,
random_state=1)

# Fit standardizer to training set

standardizer.fit(features_train)

# Apply to both training and test
sets

features_train_std                       =
standardizer.transform(features_trai
n)

features_test_std                        =
standardizer.transform(features_test
)
```

K-fold CV is free of sampling bias, it generalizes well, and the data selection matters less; however, it has a high computational cost because the training process is repeated k times. It can get even costlier, as is the case of deep learning. For data with dependent features such as time series, cross-validation is not recommended.

Using K-fold on Time Series Data

The first step is sorting the data chronologically, so every subsequent training fold increases in size by adding the data from the next time step. The performance prediction is the mean of the outcomes across the folds. We can use Scikit-learn TimeSeriesSplit to produce folds for time series data. Here is a code snippet illustrating this:

```
from sklearn.model_selection import
TimeSeriesSplit

X = np.array([[1, 2], [3, 4], [1,
2], [3, 4]])

y = np.array([1, 2, 3, 4])

tscv = TimeSeriesSplit(n_splits=3)

for train_index, test_index in
tscv.split(X):
```

```
    print("Train:",       train_index,
"Validation:", val_index)

    X_train,          X_test       =
X[train_index], X[val_index]

    y_train,          y_test       =
y[train_index], y[val_index]

## Output

#TRAIN: [0] TEST: [1]

#TRAIN: [0 1] TEST: [2]

#TRAIN: [0 1 2] TEST: [3]
```

Nested cross-validation

If you apply the same k-Fold CV technique when optimizing your model's hyperparameters, tuning the model, and evaluating its performance, you run the risk of overfitting. You don't want to calculate your model's accuracy on the same dataset split that you used to found the model's optimal hyperparameters. This is where Nested Cross-Validation method comes in. It enables you to separate the hyperparameter tuning step from the error estimation step. This is done by nesting two k-fold cross-validation loops, namely the inner hyperparameter tuning loop and the outer error estimation loop. You can use any cross-validation methods in the inner and outer loops.

It is essential to understand that it is not sufficient to validate the model, you also need to validate the data preparation targeted at improving model performance as well as many activities around the model building process such as parameter optimization or feature engineering.

Chapter Summary

- When selecting a model, its skill, computational complexity, accuracy, speed, and scalability are among the factors to consider.
- Mode selection and evaluation are often mixed up. Model selection is all about understanding how to pick out the most suitable model for your problem while evaluation is assessing whether the model, be it an algorithm or the whole pipeline, is working as intended.
- Hold-out validation is a simple computationally cheap method of evaluating a model. However, it is susceptible to sampling bias.
  - Repeated hold-out validation avoids this bias error by repeating validation a given number of times.
- Cross-validation is the best way to assess a model's performance because it is less biased (granted it has the right value of k).

- K-fold CV evaluates a models performance quite well despite the type of data used.
  - However, when using time series data, all validation methods should maintain the temporal order of the data to gauge the model's performance accurately.

Exercises

1. What is the distinction between model selection and model evaluation?
2. Why is this distinction important?
3. What consideration should you make when selecting a model?
4. In model assessment, what role does validation play?
5. Name several validation techniques used in model evaluation.
6. Does Scikit-learn have any tools to help with validation? If so, name a few.
7. Using the MNIST, Titanic, or any other dataset you can find, apply the concepts learned in this chapter and pick an appropriate model for your dataset.

Chapter Six:
Dimensionality Reduction

Suppose you are telling your friend a story or giving them a long-winded explanation about something when they ask to get to the point of the story. It might seem rude at first but put yourself in your friend's shoes. We are all busy people with things to do, and we want our information to be fast and to-the-point. In essence, this is what dimension reduction entails. A lot of ML problems can involve anywhere from thousands to millions of features for a single training instance. When dealing with such massive data, we can use dimensionality algorithms to literally make the data get to the point.

Handling such large data not only makes training hard and incredibly slow, but it also makes it more difficult to find a good solution. This issue is referred to as the curse of dimensionality. Fortunately, we have the ability to decrease the number of features significantly when dealing with real-world problems, thus turning a complex problem into a more manageable one. For instance, in the MNIST dataset, the outlying border pixels are almost always white, so we can drop them without losing too much or any data. You can merge two neighboring pixels without losing too much information since they are closely associated.

Reducing dimensionality can cause some data loss, just like when you compress an image into a different format. As a result, the model becomes degraded. Although it quickens training, reducing dimensionality can cause the model to perform slightly worse. It can make your pipelines harder to maintain due to the increased complexity. It is advised to train your model using the original data first before reducing dimensionality because it is running slower at this point. Also note that in some cases, dimensionality reduction can help eliminate some noise and unnecessary information, thus causing the model to perform better. This, however, is a rare occurrence. What dimensionality reduction does most is speed up training.

Apart from that, dimensionality reduction is a handy data visualization tool. By reducing the number of dimensions to either three or four, models can plot a high-dimensional training set on a graph and gain meaningful insight into their program, such as seeing patterns like clusters.

Why Dimensionality Reduction is Needed

Reducing a dataset's dimensions has some advantages. This process reduces the space necessary to store data, and processing this reduced dataset takes up less computational time. It helps some algorithms perform better while handling correlated redundant features from the data. For example, say you have two features: time spent running and calories burnt. These features are correlated since the more time you run, the more calories you lose. Thus, there is no point in keeping both of these data points. Reduction also helps with data visualization. By reducing high-dimensional spaces into 2D or 3D, we can analyze the data better.

The Curse of Dimensionality

The curse of dimensionality is a term that refers to the different phenomena that occur when analyzing and classifying data in high-dimensional spaces that don't happen in low-dimension spaces, such as 2D or 3D. We are so used to living in 3D—or 4D, if you count time—that the concept of high-dimensionality eludes us. For a lot of people, simply picturing a simple 4D hypercube is difficult, let alone an ellipsoid bent in a 300-dimension space.

In essence, the curse of dimensionality refers to when your data has too many features. It is the realization that as the number of dimensions goes up, the volume on the unit space doesn't. Things tend to behave quite differently in high-dimensional space. Take, for instance, a random node in a unit square (1x1). It has about a 0.4% chance of being less than 0.001 from the border; that is, it is highly unlikely for any point to be very far from the edge in any dimension. Now in a 1,000-dimensional unit hypercube (1x1x1...x1 with a thousand ones), the chances of this are greater than 99.9999% since most points are pretty close to the border.

You could be wondering how this relates to machine learning. Suppose you've chosen two points randomly in a unit square. The distance between them would roughly be 0.5. If you did the same in a 3D cube, the distance would be 0.66. But what if you choose two random points in a 10,000-dimensional hypercube? The average distance would be 40.823 ($\sqrt{(10,000/6)}$). This result is shocking. How can two points be so far apart but still be in the same hypercube? This phenomenon represents the risk high-dimensional data points face: being sparse and far away from each other. It also means that new instances will be far from training instance, making the model's predictions less reliable than those from low-dimensional spaces. It is because they are established on larger extrapolations. In simple terms, the more the dimensions a training set has, the more likely it is that overfitting will occur.

Another potential problem of high-dimensional data is that with too many features, observations can be hard to cluster. The dimensions cause instances to appear equidistant from each other. Since clustering algorithms use a distance measure such as Euclidean distance to quantify similar observations, this presents a big problem. If all observations are equidistant, then they are alike; and thus no meaningful clusters can be formed.

Theoretically, one way to solve this curse would be to increase the training dataset size to get the optimal density of training instances required. As the number of input dimensions gets more extensive, we will need more data to enable the algorithm to generalize well. Our algorithms try to separate data into classes based on the features. Therefore, as the number of features increases, so do the number of data points we require. So, for a hundred features, you would require more training instances than the atoms in the observable universe for them to be 0.1 away from each other on average. This is assuming they are uniformly spread out across all dimensions. For this reason, we will have to be very careful about what information we input into the algorithm, meaning that we need to understand something about the data in advance.

Approaches to Dimensionality Reduction

You must understand that no fixed rule defines the number of features to use in a regression or classification model. The right number depends on the training data used, the decision boundaries complexity, and the algorithm used. Before looking at dimensionality reduction algorithms, we will first take a look at the two approaches used to decrease dimensionality, namely projection and Manifold learning.

● Projection

As stated before, training instances are never evenly spread across all dimensions when we use real-world data. You could have some constant features, and others could be highly correlated. This makes all the training instances fall within a lower-dimensional subspace of the high-dimensional space. Let's look at this example to illustrate better what this means. Suppose we have some 3D data, represented on this figure by the circles:

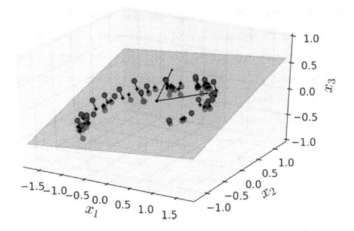

You can see that all the instances lie close to a plane, a lower 2D subspace in the 3D space. If these instances were projected perpendicularly onto the subspace, shown by the short lines connecting them, we get a new two-dimensional dataset as shown below:

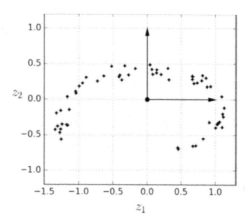

We have just reduced the data from 3D into 2D, and the axes on the graph correspond to the coordinates of the projection on the plane, z1, and z2. Unfortunately, projection isn't always the best way to deal with dimensionality reduction. In cases where the data twists and turns, merely projecting the data onto a plane would squish the various layers together instead of what you really want them to do, which is to unroll the data to get a 2D dataset.

- Manifold Learning

The case above is an excellent example of a 2D manifold. Put simply, it is a 2D shape that can be bent and twisted in a high-dimensional space. Generally, a d-dimensional manifold is a section of an n-

140

dimensional space where d < n and it looks like a d-dimensional hyperplane. A lot of dimensionality reduction models work by modeling the Manifold in training instances. This is referred to as manifold learning, which relies on the manifold hypothesis, which states that most real-world, high-dimensional datasets are all within a much lower-dimensional manifold.

If you think back to the MNIST dataset, you will notice that most of the handwritten images have similarities (they are made of connected lines, designed with white borders, they are mostly centered, etc.). If you were to generate images randomly, only a few of them would look like handwritten digits. Put differently, the freedom degrees you have when creating a digit image are significantly lower than the freedom degrees you would have if you generated any image you wanted. These constraints push the dataset into a lower-dimensional manifold.

Yet another implicit assumption usually accompanies the manifold hypothesis: the classification or regression task at hand will be more straightforward if it is conveyed in the lower-dimensional manifold space. However, this assumption doesn't always hold water as the decision boundary in lower-dimensional spaces may not always be simpler.

Now that you have a good sense of what the dimensionality curse is and how algorithms reduce it using projection and Manifold learning, we can now look at popular dimension reduction algorithms.

Principal Component Analysis (PCA)

This is the most prevalent dimension reduction algorithm used in machine learning. It begins by identifying the hyperplane closest to the data and projects the data onto it. It emphasizes variation and shows strong patterns present in a dataset. It is used to make data easy to explore and visualize. PCA transforms variables into new variables, referred to as principal components (PCs), which are orthogonal and ordered in such a way that the preservation of variance present in the original dataset reduces as you move down the order. Suppose we have a two-dimensional dataset expressed in three different axes (one-dimensional hyperplanes), as shown below:

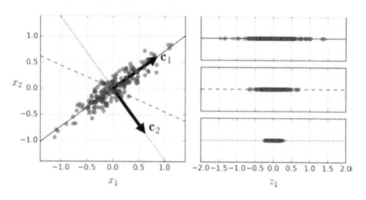

As you can see, projecting the data onto the solid line preserves the maximum variance, which gradually reduces as we project onto the dashed line, and then finally onto the dotted line. The dotted line preserves the least variance of the three lines. Therefore, it stands that the model would choose the axis that preserves the most variance because less data loss will occur during projection. You could say that it minimizes the mean squared distance between the original data and the shadow projected on said axis.

We already know that PCA picks out the axis with the maximum variance, which is a solid line in the above example. But it also finds a secondary axis orthogonal to the first one, which represents the largest amount of the remaining variance. In our example, the secondary axis is dotted line. For higher-dimensional datasets, PCA would continue finding the next orthogonal axis in as many of the dimensions in the dataset as possible. The vector unit that defines the ith axis is known as the ith PC; and in the above example, the first PC is c_1, and the second one is c_2. It is important to note that the PC directions are not stable. If you were to rerun the PCA algorithm, some of the PCs would still lie on the same axes, but would face the opposite direction than they did originally. In some instances, PCs may swap or rotate about the same axis.

To help you find the PCs of a training set, you can use a standard matrix factorization method known as singular value decomposition (SVD). It decomposes the training set matrix X into dot products of three matrices, namely $U \cdot \Sigma \cdot V^{T}$, where V^{T} has all the PCs that we need, as shown in the equation below:

$$V^{T} = \begin{pmatrix} | & | & & | \\ c_1 & c_2 & \cdots & c_n \\ | & | & & | \end{pmatrix}$$

This code uses NumPy's svd() function to get all the PCs of the training set, then extracts the first two:

```
X_centered = X - X.mean(axis=0)

U, s, V = np.linalg.svd(X_centered)

c1 = V.T[:, 0]

c2 = V.T[:, 1]
```

Important Note: PCA presumes that the dataset is centered around the origin, and Scikit-learn PCA classes automatically center this data for you. If you are implementing PCA yourself or you decide to use other libraries, remember to center the data.

Projecting Down

After identifying all of the PCs, you can reduce the dataset's dimensionality down to d dimensions by projecting it to the hyperplane specified by the first d PCs. The selection of this hyperplane ensures the most variance preservation.

Take the 3D example we used for projection. The 3D dataset was projected into 2D form through the first two PCs, thus preserving a lot of the variance. This made the 2D shadow projection look like the 3D projection. Estimate the dot product of the practice dataset matrix X by the matrix Wd, which holds the first d PCs (i.e., a matrix made up of the first d columns of VT) to project the dataset onto the hyperplane. The equation is as follows:

$$X_{d\text{-proj}} = X \cdot W_d$$

The corresponding code is as follows:

```
W2 = V.T[:, :2]

X2D = X_centered.dot(W2)
```

Now you know how to reduce any dataset's dimensionality down to a given number of dimensions and keep as much variance as possible. Scikit-learn executes PCA using SVD decomposition, and this code applies PCA to reduce the dataset's dimensionality down to 2D, and it automatically centers the data.

```
from sklearn.decomposition import PCA

pca = PCA(n_components = 2)

X2D = pca.fit_transform(X)
```

After adjusting the dataset to the PCA algorithm, you can get the PCs using the components variable, which has the principal components as horizontal vectors. For instance, the first PC is equal to pca.components_.T[:,0]). The explained_variance_ratio_ variable indicates the size of the data's variance on each axis of every PC. If we were to look at the Explained Variance (EV) ratios of the first two components of the 3D dataset, it would look like this:

```
>>>
print(pca.explained_variance_ratio_)

array([ 0.8425, 0.1463])
```

This shows that about 84% of the variance is on the first axis and 14% is on the second one. The 2% left is on the third axis, and we can assume it carries little information.

Selecting the Right Number of Dimensions

Rather than choosing a random number of dimensions to reduce down to, you should pick those that make up a large portion of the variance. However, if you are reducing data dimensionality for visualization, then two or three dimensions are fine. The code below calculates PCA without reducing data dimensionality first. Then, it identifies the dimensions needed for 95% variance preservation of the training data:

```
pca = PCA()

pca.fit(X)

cumsum                            =
np.cumsum(pca.explained_variance_rat
io_)

d = np.argmax(cumsum >= 0.95) + 1
```

You can then set n_components=d and run PCA again to perform dimensionality reduction.

There is an easier, more direct way of doing this. Rather than specifying the number of PCs you want to keep, you can set n-components to be a floating value between 0.0 and 1.0, which shows the variance ration you want to preserve.

```
pca = PCA(n_components=0.95)
```

```
X_reduced = pca.fit_transform(X)
```

You could also plot the explained variance (EV) as a function of the number of dimensions (i.e., explained variance against cumsum). The result is an elbow graph where the EV stops growing as quickly, and you can also see the number of dimensions that won't cause too much EV loss.

Compression PCA

After dimensionality reduction, the data will take up less space. For instance, if you were to apply PCA on the MNIST dataset while keeping 95% of its variance, you would find that features in every instance reduced from 784 to about 150. While most of the variance is preserved, the dataset is now less than 20% of its original size. This is a great compression ratio and it is clear how it could significantly speed up other algorithms, like an SVM classifier.

Reverse decompression of the dataset is also possible. By applying an inverse transformation of the PCA projection using inverse_transform(), we can get back the 784 dimensions. However, his will not produce the original data since some of it was lost in the 5% variance that was dropped, but it will be very similar. Reconstruction error is the mean square distance between the original and the reconstructed instances.

148

Incremental PCA (IPCA)

A drawback to the preceding PCA implementation is that all the training data should be in the machine's memory for the SVD algorithm to run. To solve this, incremental PCA was developed. It lets you split up the dataset into mini-batches and feeds them into IPCA one at a time. This method can be quite useful when processing massive datasets, and it also lets you apply PCA online or on the fly as new instances come in. The following code divides the MNIST dataset into mini-batches, using NumPy's array_split() function. These batches are then fed into Scikit-learn's incremental PCA class to reduce the dataset's dimensions to 154. As you load each mini-batch, you must call partial_fit() instead of fit(), which we used to load the whole training set. Here's the code snippet:

```
from sklearn.decomposition import
IncrementalPCA

n_batches = 100

inc_pca =
IncrementalPCA(n_components=154)

for X_batch in
np.array_split(X_mnist, n_batches):

inc_pca.partial_fit(X_batch)
```

```
X_mnist_reduced =
inc_pca.transform(X_mnist)
```

NumPy's memmap class gives a great alternative to this as it lets us manipulate a massive data array stored on the machine's hard disk like it was all in memory since it only loads the data it needs when it needs it. Memory use is easily managed, seeing how IncrementalPCA utilizes only a tiny part of the data array at a time. This way, you can use fit() as shown below:

```
X_mm = np.memmap(filename,
dtype="float32", mode="readonly",
shape=(m, n))

batch_size = m // n_batches

inc_pca =
IncrementalPCA(n_components=154,
batch_size=batch_size)

inc_pca.fit(X_mm)
```

Randomized PCA

This is another way Scikit-learn performs PCA. It is a random or stochastic algorithm that finds an estimate of the first d PCs very quickly. It has a computational complexity of $O(m \times d^2) + O(d^3)$, instead of $O(m \times n^2) + O(n^3)$, so it is a lot faster than the other algorithms when d is much smaller than n.

```
rnd_pca = PCA(n_components=154,
svd_solver="randomized")

X_reduced =
rnd_pca.fit_transform(X_mnist)
```

Kernel PCA

PCA is a linear dimension reduction method, and thus can only be applied to datasets that are linearly separable. Applying it to non-linear datasets can result in non-optimal dimension reduction. This is where kernel PCA comes in. It uses a kernel function to project a dataset into a high-dimension feature space where it is linearly separable. It is quite similar to the idea behind support vector machines. What this means is that kPCA enables us to perform complicated, nonlinear projections to reduce dimensionality. It is a great way of preserving instance clusters after projection or when unfolding data lying on a twisted manifold. For instance, this code performs kPCA on a radial bias function (RBF) using Scikit-learn's KernelPCA class:

```
from  sklearn.decomposition  import
KernelPCA

rbf_pca  =  KernelPCA(n_components  =
2, kernel="rbf", gamma=0.04)

X_reduced = rbf_pca.fit_transform(X)
```

Since kPCA is an unsupervised learning algorithm, there are no clear performance measures that can help in selecting the optimal kernel and hyperparameter values. However, since dimension reduction is often a precursor for a supervised learning task such as classification, we can use grid search to pick the optimal kernel and hyperparameter values. For instance, this code creates a two-step pipeline, which begins by reducing dimensionality using kPCA to 2 dimensions. Then, it uses logistic regression to classify the data. Using GridSearchCV, it finds the optimal kernel and gamma value for kPCA to get the best classification in the end:

```
from sklearn.model_selection import
GridSearchCV

from sklearn.linear_model import
LogisticRegression

from sklearn.pipeline import
Pipeline

clf = Pipeline([

("kpca", KernelPCA(n_components=2)),

("log_reg", LogisticRegression())

])

param_grid = [{
```

```
"kpca__gamma":        np.linspace(0.03,
0.05, 10),

"kpca__kernel": ["rbf", "sigmoid"]

}]

grid_search      =      GridSearchCV(clf,
param_grid, cv=3)

grid_search.fit(X, y)
```

Through the best_params_ variable we can get the ideal kernel and hyperparameter values:

```
>>> print(grid_search.best_params_)

{'kpca__gamma':
0.043333333333333335,
'kpca__kernel': 'rbf'}
```

There are plenty of dimension reducing algorithms, and we cannot look at them all here. However, here are some of the more noteworthy examples:

- t-Distributed Stochastic Neighbor Embedding (t-SNE)

This reduces dimensionality by trying to keep instances that are similar to each other close and dissimilar instances apart. It is mostly used for data visualization, particularly to visualize variable clusters in high-dimensional space such as visualizing the MNIST dataset in 2D. This allows us to search for patterns in a non-linear way. However, this algorithm does have some drawbacks, such as loss of large-scale data and slow computational time. It also lacks the ability to represent large datasets meaningfully.

- Linear Discriminant Analysis (LDA)

This is a classification algorithm that learns the most discriminative axes between the classes during training. These axes can then be used to establish a hyperplane where the data can be projected. The advantage of this algorithm is that it keeps classes as far apart as possible, so it is a good dimensionality reduction method to use before running another classifier such as an SVM classifier. It doesn't maximize explained variance like PCA but instead maximizes class separability. Since it is a form of supervised ML learning, it can sometimes improve the algorithm's predictive performance, and it also has variants that can deal with specific problems. Some of its drawbacks include its ability to only work on labeled data, and the dataset has to be normalized first. New features are not interpreted easily, and you must manually set the number of components to keep.

• Locally linear embedding (LLE)

This is powerful manifold learning. Non-linear dimensionality reduction method doesn't rely on projections like the other algorithms. It works by first measuring how each training instance relates to its closest neighbor linearly. It then searches for a lower dimension shadow of the training set where these relationships are best preserved. This makes it ideal for unrolling twisted manifolds. You can implement LLE using Scikit-learn's LocallyLinearEmbedding class. This implementation makes use of the following for computational complexity: $O(m \log(m)n \log(k))$ for locating the k-nearest neighbors, $O(mnk^3)$ for weight optimization, and $O(dm^2)$ for creating the lower-dimensional spaces. Unfortunately, the m^2 makes this algorithm scale poorly when dealing with massive datasets.

Chapter Summary

- We defined what dimensionality is, how it affects datasets, and why we should reduce dataset dimensionality.
- We also defined what the curse of dimensionality is.
- We discussed the various approaches to dimension reduction, namely projection and Manifold learning.

- We delved into the various dimensionality reduction algorithms such as PCA, LLE, t-SNE, LDA, and more.
- While we learned that PCA is the most popular dimension reduction algorithm, and that it has several variants. These include IPCA, Randomized PCA, and kernel PCA.
- We saw how PCA's dimension reduction also compresses data.

Exercises

1. Why is it important to reduce your dataset dimensionality?
2. What are the disadvantages of dimensionality reduction?
3. What is the dimensionality curse?
4. After reducing a dataset's dimensionality, can you reverse this transformation? If so, how do you do it? If not, explain why.
5. Can principal component analysis (PCA) be used in the dimensionality reduction of a non-linear dataset?
6. Let's say that you perform PCA on a 10,000-dimensional dataset with an explained variance ratio of 95%. How many dimensions will the output dataset have?
7. In what instances would you use Incremental PCA, Randomized PCA, or Kernel PCA? Provide an example for each.

8. How can you gauge a dimensionality reduction algorithm's performance on your dataset?

9. Can you chain two different dimensionality reduction algorithms? Should you do this? If so, why?

10. Load a dataset and split it into a training set and a test set.

    a. Train an SVM classifier on the dataset and record how long it takes. Then evaluate the output on the dataset.

    b. Use PCA to decrease the data's dimensionality with an EV ratio of 95%. Train a new SVM classifier on the reduced dataset and record how long it takes. Was it faster?

    c. Assess the classifier on the test set and see how it compares to the previous SVM classifier.

11. Use any of the algorithms to visualize the MNIST dataset after reducing it to about 2D and plot the output using Matplotlib. Now try using other dimensionality reduction algorithms and compare the resulting visualizations.

Chapter Seven:
Artificial Neural Networks

Many great inventions have been inspired by nature—birds inspired us to want to fly and an apple inspired us to track gravity. It stands to reason that we would look to nature, specifically to the human brain, when trying to build an intelligent machine. This is what inspired the development of artificial neural networks (ANNs). That said, planes don't flap their wings to fly because they were inspired by birds. Likewise, ANNs have changed and are now vastly different from their biological counterparts. Artificial neural networks are at the epicenter of deep learning because they are robust, powerful, versatile, and scalable. All of these traits make them ideal when handling massive and complex ML problems. These include classifying images (e.g. Google photos), speech recognition (e.g. Siri, Alexa, or Google Assistant), or making recommendations on sites (e.g. YouTube or Amazon), and so on. In this chapter, we will introduce neural networks, their various architectures, and their importance.

What are Artificial Neural Networks?

Artificial Neural Networks are computing systems composed of several simplistic, highly interconnected processing units that process data from the input to output space. Put differently, it is a computational system that uses a network of functions to understand inputted data and translate it into the desired output, which is usually in another form. As stated before, these nets are a set of algorithms that are modeled after the neuron structure of the human brain and how neurons work together to interpret sensory data. Whereas a massive artificial network has hundreds or thousands of processing units or neurons, the brain has numerous neurons with a corresponding increase in the magnitude of their overall interaction and emergent behavior.

ANNs are one of the many methods used in machine learning algorithms, as the network can be utilized as a piece in several algorithms to process complex data into an output space that the machine can understand. They are designed to identify patterns, often represented in numerical form, into which all data must be translated to; this includes real-world data containing images, text, or categorical data,.

Neural Networks help us classify and cluster data. Think of them as a cluster or classification layer on top of the data stored and controlled by the system. They group unlabeled data as per their similarities with training data examples and classify them to the labels. They can also extract features fed to other algorithms for clustering and classification. Think of deep Neural Networks as parts of a larger ML model containing algorithms from reinforcement learning, classification, and regression.

ANNs strive to provide and process data the same way the brain would. Every neuron or node receives a large number of inputs, and functions are applied to them, which results in the activation of node levels, which contain the neuron output. In an artificial neural network, there is dynamic connectivity, and thus the computation is collective. The memory is short-term, internalized, and distributed. They also have redundancies and shared responsibilities. These neural networks are used when the rules are unknown or complex, or if the data is too noisy or incomplete.

A neural network is made up of a neuron—which is the data processing unit of the network—and a neural network architecture—which is how the neurons are connected and a learning algorithm used to train the net.

How Neural Networks Work

The billions of neurons in our brains process information in the form of electrical signals. A stimulus is received in the dendrites, processed in the neuron body, and transformed into an output that is passed through the axon to the next neuron. Here, it can choose whether to accept or reject it, depending on the signal strength. Artificial neural networks also work similarly. A neuron combines data input with a set of coefficients (referred to as weights) to either amplify or dampen the data input. This assigns significance to the data input with regard to what the algorithm is trying to learn (e.g. which input is most helpful when classifying data). The input-weight products are summed, and the result is passed to the next node through an activation function. This function determines whether and to what extent the signal should travel through the network. This ultimately affects the overall outcome, which is the classification action. If the signals pass through a neuron, it is considered activated. Here is what a basic artificial neuron looks like:

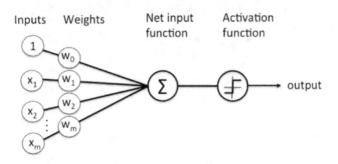

ANNs are organized in layers made up of several interconnected neurons that contain an activation function. Patterns are then presented to the network through the input layer with communicates with other hidden layers, where the actual processing is done. These hidden layers then link to the output layer that shows the result of the task. Most neural networks have a learning rule that modifies the connection weights as per the input patterns they are shown. In essence, ANNs learn by example, just like their biological counterparts. Think of how a child learns to do and recognize things from examples.

For instance, suppose there is a financial institution that wants to gauge whether it should approve a customer's loan application. It wants to know if the client is likely to default on the loan or not. Here is a table showing the data the bank has:

Customer ID	Customer Age	Debt Ratio (% of Income)	Monthly Income ($)	Loan Defaulter Yes:1 No:0 (Column W)	Default Prediction (Column X)
1	45	0.80	9120	1	0.76
2	40	0.12	2000	1	0.66
3	38	0.08	3042	0	0.34
4	25	0.03	3300	0	0.55
5	49	0.02	63588	0	0.15
6	74	0.37	3500	0	0.72

We want the system to predict data for column X with a prediction close to 1, indicating that the customer has a higher chance of defaulting. Here is a simple network architecture to show what this processing data would look like this:

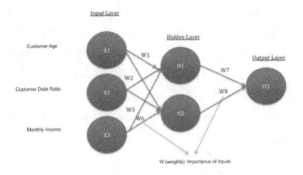

O3 indicates the outcome of the task, i.e., the default probability.

Here are some key points we can derive from this example:

This net has an input layer, a hidden layer (there can be more than one), and an output layer, and it is referred to as an MLP (multilayer perceptron). The hidden layer acts as a distillation layer as it selects which signals to pass on and which to kill off. This makes the network work faster and more efficiently by recognizing which information is important and leaving the redundant information out. The activation function captures the non-linear relationship between the input and helps transform the input into a more useful output. In the above illustration, the activation function used was a sigmoid function because it creates output values between 0 and 1: (O1 = 1 / (1+exp(-F)), where F = W1*X1 + W2*X2 + W3*X3). Other activations functions such as Tanh, RELU, and

Softmax can be used. The hidden layer leads to the final prediction: $O3 = 1 / (1+\exp(-F\ 1))$, where $F\ 1 = W7*H1 + W8*H2$. The output value predicted is between 0 and 1. The weight represents the input's importance—if w1 is 0.4 and w2 is 0.8, then higher importance is given to x2: debt ratio than x1: age in h1's prediction.

This is referred to as a feed-forward network because all the input signals are flowing in one direction: from input to output. There are other networks where the data flows in both directions known as feed-back networks. A good model with high accuracy will give predictions that come close to the actual values. In our example, column X values come very close to column W, and the difference in these values is the error in prediction. To get a good model that makes accurate predictions, you need to find the optimal values of the weights (W) that reduce the prediction error of the model. You can achieve this by using the backpropagation algorithm, and thus the network learns from the errors and improves itself.

Backpropagation

Backpropagation implements a gradient descent inside the prediction's vector space towards a global minimum along the steepest vector of the prediction error surface. Picture the error surface as a hyper paraboloid whose surface is very irregular, and this can cause the algorithm to settle on the local minimum, which is not the ideal solution.

Since it is impossible to know the nature of the error space beforehand, neural network analysis often requires a lot of training runs to ascertain the best solution. Most learning rules have built-in mathematical terms to help in this process, which controls the rate of learning (i.e., the speed and momentum). The learning speed refers to the convergence rate between the current prediction and the global minimum. The learning momentum helps the network overcome obstacles such as the local minima in the error curve to get as close to the global minimum as it can.

Once you are satisfied with how well your neural network is trained, it can be used as an analytical tool on other datasets. With ANNs, you don't have to specify any training runs. Instead, allow the network to work in forward-propagation mode only. New data is inputted and filtered and processed by the middle or hidden layers, just like with the training sets. However, the output here is preserved and no backpropagation takes place. The product of a forward propagation run is the predicted algorithm for the data, which can then be used for additional analysis and interpretation.

Neural networks can be overtrained. This means that the net has been trained to respond to a particular type of input, which is similar to rote memorization. If this happens, then the network can no longer learn. This is not ideal in real-world applications because you would have to separate these networks for every new kind of input.

How ANNs Differ from Conventional Computing Methods

To better grasp artificial neural computing, we must first understand how a conventional serial computing system processes data. A serial computer has a CPU that can locate data and make computations by reading instructions and any data the task needs from storage. Then, this command is run and the output is saved in a specified location. In a serial computing system, the computational steps are sequential and logical, and you can track a variable's state as it moves from one operation to the next.

In comparison, ANNs are not sequential, nor do they contain any complex CPUs. Instead, numerous simple processing units take the weighted sum of their inputs from other processors. These networks don't run programmed commands either. Instead, they respond in correspondence (either simulated or actual) to the pattern of presented data. The information output is not stored in a separate location. It is contained in the overall activation state of the network. Insight is thus described by the network itself, which is quite literally the summation of its components.

You might be wondering where neural networks could be used. To answer that, you must understand that neural networks are universal approximators and that they run best if the system you are using to model them has a high error tolerance. So using them to balance your checkbook is a definite no-no. However, they work very well for recognizing relationships or identifying regularities in a set of patterns where the amount, number of variables, or variety of the input is very high. Neural networks are best when applied to cases where the correlations between variables are either vaguely understood or hard to define using conventional approaches.

Depending on the use and the strength of the internal input patterns, you can generally expect ANNs to train quite well. This pertains to problems where the connections may be dynamic or nonlinear. ANNs present an analytical option to conventional methods, which are restricted by strict presumptions of normality, linearity, variable independence, and so on. An ANN's ability to recognize many different types of relationships between input variables allows the user to swiftly and efficiently model phenomena which would have otherwise been very hard or nearly impossible to tell otherwise.

Neural Network Architectures

Neural nets can be classified into the following categories:

1. Feed-Forward Neural Networks

These are the most prevalent type of neural nets utilized in practical applications. Their basic structure is an input layer, a hidden layer, and an output layer. If they contain more than one hidden layer, they are referred to as deep neural networks. They calculate a series of conversions that alter the similarities between cases. The actions of the neurons in a particular layer are a nonlinear function of those in the underlying layer.

2. Recurrent Neural Networks (RNNs)

These networks have guided cycles in their connection graph. This means that you can sometimes go back to where you started in the net by following the arrows. RNNs are known to have complex dynamics that make then biologically realistic, but this also makes them very challenging to train. Since RNNs are biologically realistic, they are a natural way of processing and modeling sequential data. Their structure is very similar to deep nets with a hidden layer per time slice. The difference is that they use the same weights at each time slice and they get input at each slice. A lot of energy has gone into finding effective ways of training RNNs, since they can remember information in their hidden state for long periods. Still, it is tough to train them to use this potential.

3. Symmetrically Connected Networks

They are similar to recurrent networks, but the links between units are symmetrical (they have the same weight in both directions). Symmetric systems are easier to analyze than recurrent networks. However, they are also more restricted in terms of what they can do because they obey an energy function. Symmetrically connected nets without hidden units are known as Hopfield Nets, while those with hidden units are called Boltzmann machines.

Perceptrons

Perceptrons are regarded as the first generation of neural networks, which are simple computational models of a single neuron. Frank Rosenblatt, an American scientist who made major contributions to the study of AI in the 1950s, initially developed the perceptron. It is also referred to as a feed-forward neural network because the information flows in one direction, from the front to the back. To train these types of neural nets, you need to use backpropagation, giving it paired datasets of inputs and outputs. The input data that is sent to the neuron, transformed, and output is the result of this transformation. The backpropagated error is the difference between the input and the output data. With enough hidden layers, the network can always model the connection between input and output. Their use is more limited, but they are usually combined with another network to create new neural nets.

A perceptron with more than three layers is referred to as a multilayer perceptron network. They are used to classify data that cannot be separated linearly. This network is known as a fully connected network because every node in a layer is linked to every node in the next layer. This neural net uses a non-linear activation function, such as either a hyperbolic or logistic tangent function, to process the data. These networks are used extensively in speech recognition models and in machine translation technologies. Here is an example of what a multilayer perceptron network looks like:

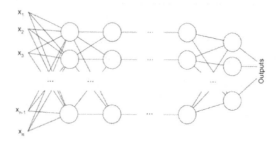

If you select enough features by hand, you can do just about anything with your perceptron network. For binary data vectors, you can have separate feature units for each of the exponentially numerous binary vectors, and you can make any possible discrimination for the data vectors. Perceptrons do have certain drawbacks. For instance, once the hand-coded features have been defined, there are extreme limitations on what a neural network can learn.

Convolutional Neural Networks (CNN)

In 1998, Yann LeCun—a French-American scientist the current Director of AI Research at Facebook—and his collaborators developed LeNet, a recognizer for handwritten digits that utilized backpropagation in a feed-forward network with several hidden layers. It also contained many maps of replicated features in each layer and output pooling of nearby replicated features. It was a wide neural net that could cope with many characters simultaneously, even if they overlapped; and it had a clever way of training a complete model, not just a recognizer. This network would later be formalized and renamed as convolutional neural networks (CNNs).

A convolutional neural network is a modification of the multilayer perceptrons network framework, containing one or more convolutional layers. These layers can either be wholly interconnected or pooled.

Before the output is passed to the following layer, the convolutional layer applies a convolutional operation on the input. This convolutional operation can make the network deeper with very few input parameters.

CNNs are considerably different from most other networks. They are primarily used for image processing and classification, but they can also be used for other kinds of input, such as audio or text. They have also shown excellent results in semantic parsing and paraphrase detection. A typical example of their use is in classifying images. They begin by scanning the input data, but not to parse it. For instance, if you wanted to input an image of 300x 300 pixels, you wouldn't want a layer with 90,000 nodes. Instead, you would make a scanning input layer of, let's say, 30 x 30 and feed in the first 30 x 30 pixels. Once it has passed, you feed it the next 30 x 30 pixels by moving the scanning unit two pixels to the right.

This input is fed through convolutional layers, where not all neurons are connected, rather than regular layers. Each neuron only cares about the neighboring cells (the cells that are close to it). These convolutional layers shrink as they become deeper, mostly by easily divisible factors of the input. These layers also feature pooling layers as a way of filtering out details. A common pooling method is max pooling where we take, for instance, 3 x 3 pixels and pass on the next pixel with the most red.

Recurrent Neural Networks (RNNs)

In this network, the output of a particular layer is saved and fed back as the input, thus helping predict the most probable outcome of the layer. Here, the input layer is formed just like in a feed-forward network (i.e., with the product of the summation of the weights and features). In the following layers, however, the recurrent neural network process begins.

As we move from one time-step to another, the next neuron will remember a bit of the previous time-step information. Simply put, each neuron acts as a memory cell while the network computes and carries out operations. The neural net starts with the front propagation as routine but retains the information it may need to use later on. If a wrong prediction is made, the system learns on its own and strives to make the right prediction during backpropagation. This makes it very useful in text-to-speech translation technology.

To understand RNNs, we need a brief overview of sequence modeling. When implementing machine learning to sequences, we want to turn an input sequence into an output sequence that exists in a different region—turning a series of sound pressures into a sequence of word characters, for instance. Without a separate target sequence, we can get a training signal by trying to foretell the next term in the input sequence. The target output sequence then becomes the input sequence with the next step. This seems more natural than trying to predict one piece of an image from the rest of the picture. Predicting the next part in a sequence obscures the distinction between supervised and unsupervised learning. It applies methods intended for supervised learning, but it doesn't need a separate teaching signal.

Memoryless models are used to tackle such a task. Autoregressive models in particular can predict what comes next in a sequence from a set number of preceding terms using delay taps. Feed-forward nets are general autoregressive models that utilize one or several layers of non-linear hidden units. However, if we assigned the model a hidden state and gave this hidden state some internal dynamics, we would get a more interesting model that stores data in its hidden state longer. Knowing the exact state of the model's hidden state can be difficult if its dynamics and output generation are noisy.

RNNs are powerful because they have a distributed hidden state that enables them to store a lot of output data and non-linear dynamics that permit updates of their hidden state in complex ways. Given enough neurons and time, you can compute anything using RNNs. RNNs can oscillate, settle to point attractors or behave chaotically. They also have the potential to learn and implement many small programs that each retain some data and run in correspondence, interacting to generate complex effects.

A big issue that RNNs face is the vanishing gradient problem. This is where, dependent on the activation functions implemented, data is rapidly lost over time. Normally, this wouldn't be a big deal since these are just weights and not neuron states. However, the weights are actually where past data is stored through time. The former state won't be very informative if it reaches a value of zero or 1,000,000. RNNs can be used for most types of data that don't have a timeline, such as non- audio or video information that can be rendered as a sequence. An image or a text string can be inputted one pixel or character at a time, so time-dependent weights are used for what came before in the sequence rather than what occurred seconds back. Generally, recurrent nets are ideal for advancing or completing information, such as in autocompletion.

Long/Short Term Memory solved the problem RNNs had of remembering things long-term. LSTMs combat the vanishing gradient problem by adding gates and a clearly-designated memory cell. This cell stores the previous data and retains it until a forget gate tells the cell to disregard those values. They also have an input gate that adds new information into the memory cell and an output gate that determines when to output vectors from the memory cell to the next hidden state.

Remember that with all recurrent nets, the values coming in from input layers are used to decide what happens in the present hidden state. The outcome of the current hidden state is used to define what occurs in the next hidden state. LSTMs include a memory cell layer to ensure that the transfer of hidden state data from one repetition to the next is reasonably high. In other words, we want to recall data from earlier repetitions for as long as we need to, and LSTMs memory cells allow this to happen; and they can also learn complex sequences.

Deep Belief Networks (DBFs)

A deep-belief network is defined as a stack of restricted Boltzmann machines (RBM) where every RBM layer interacts with both the previous and succeeding network layers, but the neurons of any single layer don't interact with each other laterally. This RBM stack might end with a Softmax layer to build a classifier, or it can help in clustering unlabeled data in an unsupervised learning model. In a DBF, all layers except for the first and last ones have a double role: they serve as hidden layers to the previous neurons and as the input layer to subsequent neurons. Think of DBFs as nets built of single-layer neural networks.

176

They are used to identify, cluster, and create images, video sequences, and even motion-capture data. A continuous deep-belief network is an extension of a DBF that receives a continuum of decimals, rather than binary data. There are many neural net types, each with a different variation or combination of several of the networks we've looked at. For instance, sequence-to-sequence models are comprised of two RNNs.

Chapter Summary

- We defined what artificial neural networks are and how they work.
  - They are modeled after the brain's neuron structure and they mimic how the brain processes data.
- We also discussed how they differ from serial computing methods and their various applications.
- There are several neural network architectures from perceptrons to CNNs, DBFs and RNNs. Each has its advantages and drawbacks, making their applications and uses quite different.

Exercises

1. Can you name other ANN architectures?
2. What is the best neural net for image classification?

3. What is a pooling layer, and why do you need it?

4. If you were to tackle the MNIST dataset, which neural net architecture would you use?

5. Can you combine a convolutional neural network with an RNN to classify videos? How would you do this?

6. What are LSTMs? How are they used in RNNs?

Final Words

In this book, we delved deeper into machine learning; from reminding ourselves of the fundamentals of machine learning to learning new things, such as how to handle data in ML systems, classification, dimensionality, and more. Machine learning is at the helm of many of the data processing that takes place today, and it has helped us discover and learn things we never would have seen otherwise. The numerous applications of machine learning models have revolutionized how we think, shop, trade, invest, and even diagnose diseases.

Take image processing and character recognition using artificial neural networks, for instance. They are a great example of the power of machine learning, given their ability to take in a lot of inputs and process them to identify hidden as well as complex, nonlinear relationships. Character recognition, such as in handwriting, has a variety of applications in fraud detection (especially in banks) and even national security assessments. Image recognition is a continuously growing field with many applications, including facial recognition in social media or photo repositories, cancer detention, and satellite imagery processing for agricultural and defense usage. Research on the application of neural networks in ML has paved the way for deep nets that constitute the basis of deep learning, which has now opened up exciting and transformational discoveries in computer vision, speech recognition, natural language processing and, in more recent years, self-driving cars.

More and more people like yourself are interested in learning more about the technology behind so many complex processes that have become easier thanks to machine learning. This book is intended to be a beginner's guide to machine learning, but it's also for anyone interested in machine learning, not just beginners. The examples, images, and exercises are meant to help you grasp the concepts taught in every chapter. And while it might take time before you are a pro, reading this book is a step in the right direction.

Image Credit: Shutterstock.com